Driving to
L and Back

Driving to
L and Back

God Bless Our Learner Drivers

[signature]

P.W. Wolfendale

Illustrations by David Booth

authorHOUSE®

AuthorHouse™
1663 Liberty Drive
Bloomington, IN 47403
www.authorhouse.com
Phone: 1-800-839-8640

Published by AuthorHouse   10/05/2012

ISBN: 978-1-4772-3393-1 (sc)
ISBN: 978-1-4772-3394-8 (e)

Contents

Acknowledgements

The hilarious stories in this book are all thanks to my amazing pupils, examiners and driving instructors. Without their input this book would still be just a pipe dream. I did quite a lot of research by talking to these people about writing this book and was overwhelmed by their response. Yes yes they all said, a great idea, can't wait to read it, so I would like to thank you one and all for your invaluable feedback. A special thanks goes to all my family for being so understanding, I didn't realise how grouchy I became whilst writing this book. I would come home from a hard day's work and then get stuck in to writing this book without much thought for their feelings. My family mean a lot to me, so I would like to give them a mention. My wife Julia, Daughters Emily Tatiana and Melanie, and my son Joshua. My wife and Emily helped me with their constructiveness of this book, Emily also supplied four of the illustrations No1 No4 No6 and No30.

Introduction

Welcome to *Driving to L and Back*, an amazing book of true facts compiled from over twenty years' experience as a driving instructor. Never before have tales like these been compiled for human consumption. This book tells behind-the-scenes stories from inside the driving instructor's car, things you will find hard to believe. Over the last twenty years as a driving instructor I have seen so many changes in the way the driving test has changed. Theory tests, independent driving, show me/tell me questions, even examiners with a sense of humour all these topics are exposed in the contents of this hilarious book. With full of black and white illustrations highlighting the wonderful text, you will not want to put this book down until you have read the whole thing. I would like to ensure everyone that no animals were used as extras in the making of this book. The ones that were killed died due to no fault of mine or my pupils. Also to prevent any embarrassment to any of my pupils, any names I have used are all fictitious, even though my pupils have earned the right to be part of this book. I hope you have as much fun reading this book as I did writing it.

1

Holy Cow

Whilst driving along a busy, single-carriageway road, my seventeen-year-old pupil noticed a red triangular road sign with a picture of a cow inside the triangle. Underneath the sign, attached to the post, were two lights one at the top of the post and one halfway down. My pupil then asked me a question: "What does that sign mean? And what are the lights on the post for?" I replied, "A red triangular sign is a warning sign, and the cow in the triangle is a symbol for cattle, so it is warning you of cattle in the road ahead. The lights on the post will also flash to give you prior warning of any cattle that might be crossing in the road ahead."

About thirty seconds passed in which the pupil must have been thinking about the answer I had given her. She replied with a kind of confused voice, "How do the cows know when to cross?" I had to get her to repeat the question, as I was somewhat confused. She repeated the same question: "How do the cows know when to cross?" Trying not to laugh, I just sat motionless for a while. Then I said to her, "The cows do not cross on their own. A farm worker comes along and activates the lights with some sort of key, and then, when it was safe, he escorts the cattle across the road." The pupil, still looking confused, accepted the answer by saying, "Ohhhhh!"

To this day I still have my doubts as to whether she understood the answer.

2

Greek Mythology

I was teaching a Greek pupil once, and although he was a great person and a wonderful driver, the language barrier was always a slight problem. His English was good at times, however he never really understood driving instructions all that well. I had just completed the roundabout brief, then double checked to see he had understood everything we had covered.

"Yes," he said, "I understand."

We started off by negotiating a few simple left turns and then we got on to doing some straight-ahead instructions. After we had gone around several roundabouts everything seemed to be going fine, and I was praising him for the standard he was driving at. Thinking everything was going well, I decided to get him to turn right at the next roundabout. On approach, my instruction was "At the roundabout, I would like you to turn right." As there were only three exits off the roundabout, one on the left and one straight ahead, there seemed no need to explain that it was the third exit off the roundabout.

After entering the roundabout my pupil drove around the roundabout and past the exit he was expected to come off at. I kept quiet to see what his next move was, and to my amazement he continued to drive past the exit for a second time, then a third time. I was starting to get a little dizzy now and was also becoming a little disorientated.

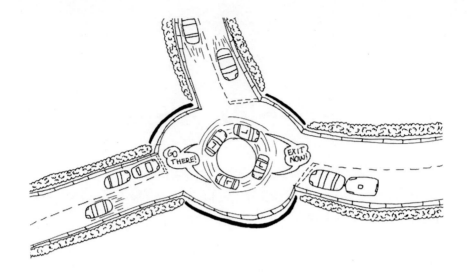

Thinking this guy was taking the piss, I decided it was about time I put a stop to this before I went crazy. I told him in a very polite and calm voice, "Please take the next exit off the roundabout." After exiting the roundabout we pulled over at the side of the road (at least I think it was the side of the road my head was still spinning), and I said to him, "Why didn't you come off the roundabout at the third exit as instructed.

He replied, in a Greek accent "You said right at the roundabout, but you didn't say which exit to come off at, so I keep driving around the roundabout until you tell me come off."

I was in total disbelief, as I thought to myself, "Is this guy serious?" After I explained to him where he had gone wrong, he started to laugh and said he was sorry. "I will remember next time to exit the roundabout."

3

Turkish Delight

Whilst driving towards a major T junction with my Turkish pupil, it suddenly dawned on me that he was not slowing down. I didn't want to over-instruct him, as his driving was at quite a good standard and he was more than capable of negotiating a T junction. As we got closer to the junction, it was becoming obvious he was not going to stop or even slow down. My wife and kids flashed through my mind as I was thinking I might not see them again. It was now time for me to intervene. I braced myself for some heavy braking and shouted very loudly, "Speed," thinking he would respond by braking. Not a chance. Speed to him meant go faster, so he put the pedal to the metal. Fearing for my life, I carried out the emergency stop exercise with my dual-control brake. We stopped with half the car over the stop line.

If there had being another vehicle coming along the main road, we would have been splattered. I took a deep breath and asked him, "Why did you put us both in danger? Why did you accelerate like you did?"

His reply was "You say speed, I go faster," and he laughed. "Ha ha ha!"

I have a sense of humour like most people, but I didn't find it funny at all. I said to him that anyone with any common sense would have understood what I meant. We both agreed that in the interest of public safety it would be best if he found another driving instructor who shared the same sense of humour as him.

I never saw him again, until one day, when I was at the test centre with my pupil. He had passed his driving test. I spoke to his instructor, who had taught him after we had parted company, and she said, "I can't believe he has passed." I thought the idea of having to take a driving test was to *keep danger off the road*. Well, I'm afraid this one slipped through the net.

4

Mistaken Identity

I received a phone call one evening from another driving instructor, a friend of mine, asking me if I could take on a new pupil that he was not able to take for personal reasons. He said that the pupil was booked in for his lesson the next morning at nine o'clock. He also said that the pupil's surname was different from his mum's surname, so I shouldn't be misled by the two different names when I called to confirm his lesson. I agreed to take the pupil on board and phoned up the pupil later on that day. A well-spoken lady answered the phone without giving me her name.

I said, "Could I speak to Peter, please?"

The reply was "He is not in at this moment in time. Who's speaking, please?"

"It's the driving instructor, and I am just confirming with you that I have Peter booked in for his driving lesson tomorrow morning."

"Oh yes, that is correct. I am his mum," she replied. We never did establish each other's name, as we ended the conversation with "Look forward to seeing Peter tomorrow morning then. Bye for now."

On arriving at Peter's address, the first thing I noticed was the size of his house or should I say mansion. It was huge, with about ten or more cars parked in the grounds. I climbed the four or five concrete steps up to the door, which made me feel like a dwarf, knocked on the door, and within seconds was greeted by a lady dressed in a dressing gown, who proceeded to say with a firm handshake, "Ahh, Tyler, nice to meet you."

At this moment, the first thing that came to my mind was that her name was Tyler. I introduced myself as Paul and was invited into her house. We seemed to be walking around for ages from room to room, thinking to myself that if I was on my own I would have needed a sat-nav to find my way around. We finally reached her Kitchen. It was huge, just like all the other rooms in her house. Breakfast was cooking, and the smell of bacon was making my mouth water. I thought maybe there might be a bacon sandwich in it for me while I waited for her son.

I was invited over to where the bacon and all other goodies were cooking, and the smell was gorgeous. I could sense a bacon sandwich was not far away, but then, out of the blue, I was asked, "What do you think about all the tiles on the wall and on the worktops, Paul?"

I replied, "Yes, they are very nice looking tiles."

She then took me away from all the goodies that were cooking and on a tour of her kitchen. About ten minutes later we arrived at the other end of her kitchen. Whilst still admiring all the worktops and walls, I found it strange to say the least that she wanted me to take such an interest in her wall tiles. She then said to me, "Could you fit the whole kitchen out with the same tiles?"

It was only then that the penny dropped. I said to the lady, "Do you know who I am?"

She replied, "Yes, the tiler, aren't you?"

"No," I replied, "I am the driving instructor." Her face was a picture. I said, "I thought your name was Tyler."

"Oh, my God," she said. "I thought you were the tiler coming to tile my kitchen."

"I thought it was strange that you were asking me about the kitchen tiles."

"I am so sorry," she said, "you must think I have gone mad."

"No," I said, "this sort of thing happens to me all the time not a problem."

Her husband then entered the kitchen to the sight of his wife and myself standing next to each other sharing a few giggles. I quickly explained to him about the misunderstanding before he got the wrong idea about what was going on. Her husband doubled up with laughter.

When he finally stopped laughing, he said, "You must forgive my wife. She gets like this at weekends when she is not working."

And no, sadly, I never did get a bacon sandwich.

5

Going Continental

On a pupil's first lesson, if they have never driven before, I would normally take them to a quiet country road away from busy traffic. After explaining all the controls of the car and briefing the pupil on moving away and stopping, we then get the car moving. I was teaching this young girl all the skills needed for moving the car away under control and the stopping procedure. Her moving away and stopping skills were good for her first lesson, so i continued by teaching her how to go up and down the gears.I noticed that time was getting on, and knew that I we would not be able to go much further or I would be running over my time, so I decided to turn the car around and head back the way we came.

I explained to the pupil that because there was not a lot of time left on the lesson, we would be turning the car around and making our way back. I also explained to my pupil that I would take control of the vehicle with my dual controls so we didn't have to swap seats. When we came to a part of the road that was wide enough to complete the exercise, I said to the pupil, "Just turn the wheel to the right using the pull and push method that I have taught you, then make your way back on to your side of the road." I controlled the speed, and the pupil steered the steering wheel. Everything went well until she starting driving on the right-hand side of the road with another vehicle approaching in the distance.

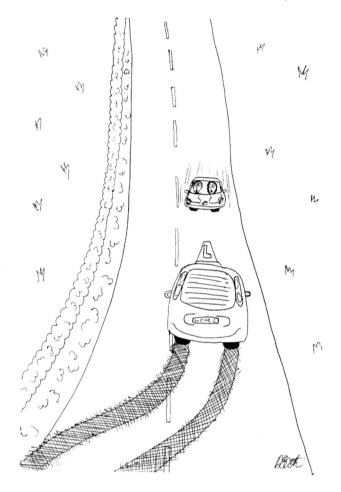

I grabbed the steering wheel and guided her back on to the left-hand side of the road. We pulled over, and then I asked her in a nice, calm voice, "Why did you position yourself on the right hand side of the road?"

She replied, "I thought the right-hand side of the road was my side of the road, because that was the side I drove up on."

This is just one of those jobs that when you go out in the morning, you don't know if you are going to return home later on that day.

6

Confused

Instructions can be confusing if not given clearly; however, I was still surprised when I said to my pupil to "release the hand brake." She was moving away under control as I talked her through the procedure. Clutch down and into gear, find the bite, keep your left foot still, cover your gas and place your hand on the hand brake, check mirrors and blind spot, set gas, and release hand brake. My pupil took her hand off the hand brake without releasing the hand brake off its ratchet. I said to the pupil, "Pardon me for what I am about to say, but why did you take your hand off the handbrake and put it onto the steering wheel?"

She replied, "You told me to release the hand brake, so I did what you said and took my hand off it." I didn't think she would take me so literally.

7

Logical Thinking (Not)

You would think that the emergency stop exercise would be a logical thing to teach early on in the first driving lesson of any pupil, so that if called upon, the pupil would be able to react unattended. Turns out this is not always a good idea. Whilst driving along a busy road in Chester at a speed of about 30 mph, my pupil noticed a vehicle travelling quite close behind us. There seemed to be no danger at all, until the vehicle behind us decided that they would overtake. Just as the vehicle moved out, my pupil noticed an oncoming vehicle and thought that the vehicle behind us would be in some sort of danger with the oncoming vehicle getting ever closer. My pupil decided to put the emergency stop exercise in to action and slammed on the brakes, nearly causing the car behind to hit the corner of my car.

P.W. Wolfendale

I don't know who was more shocked, me or the person in the vehicle behind. After scraping myself off the dashboard, we pulled over and I explained that this was not one of those occasions where the emergency stop exercise was required, the reply I got was, "I just thought I would try to put in to practice what you have taught me."

I was speechless.

8

Happy Families

Referrals are always a good way to drum up business. I think I was taking the third member of this family, which also included the girlfriend of the boy I was taking on his driving lesson on this day. It was Sunday lunchtime, the sun was shining, and I was thinking to myself what a wonderful day it was. That would soon change. I pulled up outside the pupil's house, turned off my engine, and waited for my pupil to come out of his house. Whilst waiting for him, I noticed a girl acting very suspiciously. She seemed to be hiding around the corner of the house, as if she was looking or waiting for someone. I continued observing the girls strange behaviour still trying to work out what was going on. I sat thinking to myself, something isn't quite right. Why would a girl be peering around the corner of my pupils house? I got out of my car at the same time my pupil came out of his front door. All of a sudden the girl, who I found out later was his sister, pounced on him like a tiger killing its prey and wrestled him to the ground.

I thought it was just a bit of fun at first until hostile words were exchanged in an aggressive manner. Still not sure what was going on, I just stood there watching them both grappling each other on the ground. Just then my pupil's girlfriend, whom I had taught to drive, came running out of the front door grabbing her boyfriend's sister by the hair and putting her in to a headlock. My pupil's sister then let go of her brother, and the two girls began to exchange punches before both falling to the ground and embracing in headlocks. None of them were willing to let go of each other, so my pupil decided that it was time to stick the boot in. He started kicking his sister to try to get them apart. It was like something from the hokey cokey put your left leg in, take your left leg out, in out in out in out kick you in the head.

Unfortunately it didn't work, as no one was giving an inch. I saw the pupil's mum arriving on the scene with all guns blazing.

Their mum tried to separate them without much success; all she was able to do was shout and scream at them, and all she got for her troubles was a smack in the mouth from one of the girls.

Eventually it was time for the man of the house to try his luck. He ran over to them in his string vest and managed to separate the two girls. The girl's father was able to hold on to his daughter long enough for my pupil and me to make a getaway. The last thing I saw was my pupil's sister kicking like a mule at her father's shins, screaming, "Let me go, you bar steward!" I was later to find out that the row had do with my pupil saying something about his sister's baby over Sunday lunch. On return from the driving lesson, I got my pupil to stop the car some distance from their house, just in case it all kicked off again. Luckily I never got to see his sister again. Her name was never mentioned on any further driving lessons. Maybe she has been locked up somewhere and they threw away the key.

9

Watch the Birdie

I was giving my pupil a brief on pedestrian crossings and during the recap I asked her, "What are the four types of pedestrian crossings that we commonly use?"

Zebra and pelican were the first to be mentioned, then after a short pause she managed to find one more answer: "Toucan. Is that right?"

"Yes" was my reply. "Just one more to get," I said for a full house. I could see she was struggling on the last one, so I decided to give her some help. I started by saying, "It's a type of bird."

"Still no idea."

"It begins with the letter P."

After a short pause she said, "Ah! I know what it is! It's a Pigeon crossing."

I tried my hardest not to laugh and explained to her that it was a Puffin crossing. No brownie points for you today.

10

Sticking the Boot In

Recently, the driving test has changed so that you now have to answer two questions at the beginning of your driving test before you even start the engine. The questions are all to do with the basic maintenance and the controls of your vehicle. The questions are called 'show me, tell me' questions, the examiner may ask you to show them how something works, or they may ask you to tell them how something works (e.g., "Would you show me how you would check the hand brake for excessive ware?" or "Tell me how you would operate the windscreen wipers"). I was asking my pupil where would you find the tyre pressures and how would you check the pressures of your tyres. The answer should have been that you find the pressures in the user manual, located in the vehicle, and you would then use a reliable tyre pressure gauge. Before I could blink, she started kicking the shit out of my tyre, saying that they need to be firm.

I immediately told her to stop kicking my tyre and that is not how we check the pressures! She replied, "Well, that's how my husband always does it. I have seen him do it many times."

I found it hard to believe that she thought this is how you check your tyres. I am just glad I didn't ask her how you would check the headlights.

11

Timberrrrrr

I was chitchatting with another driving instructor in the driving test centre one day and he was telling me that when he first started out as an instructor, he use to give himself about fifteen minutes travelling time in between each driving lesson. He said that after a while he found it difficult to get to the next pupil on time and was always late. This one day, whilst running a little late he asked his pupil if he knew the shorter way back to his house along the back roads, to which his pupil replied, "Yes, no problem." The instructor then said to his pupil just follow the road ahead until he was told to turn. He looked down at his diary to see who his next pupil was and how long it would take to get to him when he was thrown forward with some force to the sound of the car hitting something.

The instructor said he looked up to find to his horror that the pupil had hit a tree that had been blown into the road.

The damage to the car was very severe, the entire front smashed up. On asking the pupil why he didn't stop, he replied, "You said just follow the road ahead until I tell you to turn, so I did."

12

Quick Getaway

I once had this pupil from a less affluent area who, along with many of us, was struggling to make ends meet. The pupil was well in to his driving lessons and had a test booked for in a few weeks' time. It was important that he didn't cancel any driving lessons now with his test so close. I turned up on a fine, sunny Saturday morning about nine o'clock for his driving lesson and everything seemed fine, people walking around, postmen delivering letters, and the milkman collecting his well-earned wages. I looked towards my pupil's house when I noticed that he was peeping around his curtain through the downstairs window. I then saw him open the front door of his house and slowly lean forward so he could see around the door and up in to the street. He continued looking up and down the street until the coast was clear, and then he made a 100 m dash out of his front door across his garden over the hedge, like an Olympic gold medallist. He squatted down besides the driver's door, keeping a low profile.

He slowly opened the car door and crawled in besides me, keeping his head down below the window level.

I said, "What's the rush? I am not going to leave without you."

My pupil kept looking over to where the postman and the milkman were and said, "Quick, let's go." Before I could get my seat belt on we were gone in 60 seconds.

Once out of sight from his road, we pulled over and sorted ourselves out. He then explained why there was a need for a quick getaway. The milkman was expecting to get paid; he owed him for the last two weeks and he was just going to have to wait until next week. "I need to keep my driving lessons going!" It is nice to know that I come above the milkman in the pecking order. The gentleman made the right decision, given that he passed his driving test a few weeks later, on his first attempt.

13

Follow That Bus

It is important to give the best and clearest instructions that we can as a driving instructor; however, these can easily be misinterpreted, no matter how clear you think you have made them. I was instructing an elderly lady around a complicated roundabout in the heart of Chester. The lady was quite an experience driver, albeit a little nervous. On approach to the roundabout, she said that she understood the instruction, but she got a little bit confused on the roundabout, as there were a number of different lanes. Traffic was all around us on both sides and in front of us. I was watching very carefully to ensure she kept her line in the very heavy traffic, when she suddenly said, "I am not sure which way to go."

As I was watching all the traffic around us, it was easier for me to say, "Just follow that bus, the one in front of you."

Follow that bus was not the best instruction to give to a pupil, but it was the safest at that moment. As we exited the roundabout, and before I could give her another instruction, we turned left and followed the bus in to the bus station. I could not believe what had happened. There we were on the apron in the middle of the bus station. We got some strange looks from all the bus drivers and passengers that were waiting there. I could have hidden up my own bum.

Eventually we managed to find a road to drive on. I had to be really careful from then onwards about what I would tell her to follow tractor, fire engine, police car, ambulance, prison van who knows where we could have ended up?

14

Leave Me Alone

One of my fellow instructors was telling me that he turned up at a pupil's house one morning for his pupil's driving test. We normally turn up at the pupil's house about an hour before the test to give them some driving before their test. On arrival, he parked outside the pupil's house and went to the door, rang the bell, and waited. His mum opened the door and said that she would go and get him, as he was in his bed room. After about five minutes his mum came down the stairs and said that he was refusing to come out of his bed room. He would not open his bedroom door. "Do you think you can talk to him," his mum said. "He might listen to you." The instructor went up stairs to try to talk him into opening his bedroom door, but he was having none of it

"Leave me alone. I am not coming out!"

He had locked his bedroom door and would not come out, as he was too scared to take the test. The instructor continued trying his best to talk him out of his bedroom, but to no avail. The instructor then said that time was now ticking away, so he changed his tactics. "Get your f***ing arse out here now, you little shit!" There was still no response, so it ended up with the pupil not taking his test and losing his test fee.

P.W. Wolfendale

15

Sense of Humour

I like to think I have a sense of humour. One day I was instructing a man from China. He was enjoying his driving lesson so much that he started laughing at one of my comments. He said, "Ah Paul, I like you because you got humour sense!"

I replied, "You mean a sense of humour?"

"That what I say, you have humour sense!"

I just agreed and had a little chuckle to myself.

16

What Do I Need for My Driving Test

"What do I need to bring for my driving test?" is a question I commonly get asked by my pupils. I say both parts of your driving license, theory certificate, and your appointment confirmation letter. I was talking to a driving examiner one day from one of my local test centres when he explained to me that last week he had a candidate that turned up for her test on her own, without a driving instructor. This is not uncommon, as candidates can turn up in their own car for their driving test; however, they are normally accompanied by one of their parents or a friend. After the examiner had checked the candidate's documents, he then asked her to lead the way outside. She did the eye sight test and then the examiner asked her to lead the way to her vehicle. The candidate looked a little bemused by what he had said, and she said, "I don't have a car. I thought you provided a car for me to do my test with."

The examiner explained that it is not his duty to provide a car for the candidate's driving test, but it was her responsibility. He then asked the candidate how she got to the test centre

"My mum brought me in her BMW."

The candidate phoned her mum to see if she could return with the car so she could take her driving test, but her mum explained that she was not insured to drive the BMW. The end result was that the candidate couldn't take her driving test, so she would have had to pay for a new test. When a pupil now asks me what they need for their driving test, I start of by saying a car would be a good idea. Apparently it is rare but not unheard for candidates to turn up without a car to take their driving test.

17

Just Joking

I remember chatting to a driving instructor about general driving matters and having a laugh. She was telling me about an Asian man she was teaching to drive. She had been given the pupil by the driving school she worked for and he was a partly trained pupil who had already had several hours with another driving school. She said on arrival at his house the gentleman came out to meet her as she was getting out of the car. She shook hands with him and introduced herself to the pupil.

They got into the car, whereupon they did a recap on what the pupil had covered and how many hours he had taken with his last instructor.

He said he had taken about ten hours tuition and had covered several subjects. The instructor then said, "Have you covered roundabouts, because there are a lot of roundabouts in this area for us to negotiate, or would you like me to drive you to a more suitable area?"

The pupil then said, "No problem, I have done roundabouts before. Me good driver, my instructor says."

The instructor went through the basic procedures of getting the pupil ready for driving and talking him through the moving away procedure. Everything seemed fine, until they came to the first major roundabout. Before she could take control, he flew across the roundabout at an excessive speed, almost causing the car on the right to crash in to the side of them.

"I felt shook up, so I asked him to pull over at the first available opportunity," she said.

The instructor then said in a loud but semi-calm voice, "You almost caused us to crash at the last roundabout, and you told me that you had done roundabouts before."

The pupil starting laughing saying. "No, I was only joking. I have never done roundabouts before. I like to play joke on instructor."

The instructor said in a loud voice, "I cannot believe what you have just said to me. If you want to die, why don't you just go and play on the motorway. That would do it! If you ever play a joke like that on me again you will be walking back!"

I believe the pupil stopped taking driving lessons after a while. He was last seen heading towards the motorway.

18

No Word of a Lie

I found this one hard to believe; however, it is as real as the ground I walk on. I was briefing my pupil on crossroads and traffic lights, and when I got to the part about explaining the sequence of the lights and what each light colour meant, she said that her husband had already told her what each colour meant. "Okay," I said, "that's good then. Would you like to tell me what each one means?"

I was gob smacked when she honestly believed that green means go, amber means go quickly, and red means go with caution. I said to my pupil, "Pardon me for being intrusive, but do you have a stable relationship, or do you think your husband is trying to get rid of you?"

She just laughed and said, "You might be right, you know."

19

Sign of the Time

Whilst travelling along at speeds of around 60 mph, I decided to ask my pupil, "What does that sign mean?" It was a triangular sign with the 'road narrows from both sides' symbol inside the triangle. The pupil took both hands of the steering wheel to describe the sign, causing the car to swerve violently.

I was so shocked by his actions I just didn't know what to say. I just had a silent thought to myself: *Why me?*

20

Don't Look Down

Pupils very often ask what footwear they should wear, and my answer is whatever floats your boat if you feel comfy in your footwear and you feel you can drive safely in that type of shoe, that is what you should wear. However, I don't normally get involved in any other part of their dress, unless it might cause some sort of danger, such as baggy sleeves or clothing that makes them fidgety since it needs constant adjustment. On this day my female pupil was wearing a low-cut blouse, it being a hot summer's day. Nothing wrong with that if you've only got a small chest; however, the lady in question had a rather large chest. There are small ones, large ones, and *oh my God* ones these were certainly in the latter category.

We started the lesson, and it wasn't long before we were driving in heavy town traffic. There were two lanes of traffic, and we were in the left-hand lane approaching traffic lights that had just turned to red. We stopped at the red light and applied the hand brake. I noticed a pick-up truck approaching from behind in the right hand lane. The truck pulled alongside us and just like us was waiting for the green light to come on.

The cab of the truck was a lot higher than our car, so the workmen in the truck were looking down on to our vehicle, just passing the time of day, or so I thought. It wasn't long before all the men were looking down on us with their eyes practically popping out of their heads. They must have thought it was their birthday. They couldn't keep their eyes of my pupil and her *oh my God* chest.

I didn't know what to say. My pupil noticed the workmen looking down on her and said, "Why are those men staring at us? Have I done something wrong?"

I responded, "I have no idea, and no, you have done nothing wrong. Just keep your eyes on the traffic lights."

"They're not looking at the traffic lights."

"Really," I said, "I wonder why that is."

I found it very difficult to explain to her the nature of why they were hanging out of their cab window with their mouths wide open and not looking at the traffic lights. The traffic lights eventually changed to green, to the disappointment of the workmen in the pick-up truck. I think this is the only time I have seen someone disappointed To see the traffic lights change to green

21

Question Time

My pupil asked me, "If you are reversing around a corner to the left, it is called a left reverse, is that correct?"

"Yes."

"So if you reverse around a corner to the right, what would that be called?" asked the pupil.

I tried not to smirk and said after a pause of a few seconds, I replied, "I think it would be called a right reverse."

"Oh, okay," said the pupil. "I just wondered."

22

Flashing Lights

I was doing some general theory work with my pupil whose theory test was imminent. I asked her what was meant by the flashing of headlights according to the Highway Code. The answer I was expecting was that flashing of headlights meant the vehicle was warning you of their presence. The answer I got was, "Ar, I know this one. It means that there is a speed trap ahead. The police are trying to catch someone speeding."

Where on earth could she possibly have got that idea from? Surely she wasn't telling me that all law-abiding drivers must flash their headlights to warn other drivers that there is a police speed trap ahead.

On another occasion I was talking to a driving instructor in the test centre when he told me about a driving lesson where his pupil noticed an emergency vehicle behind them with their blues and twos on. The instructor said, "I explained to the pupil that you must pull over when it is safe to do so without causing any unnecessary inconvenience to other road users. On the day of her driving test, she was confronted with the same situation. She noticed an emergency vehicle behind her, so i instructed her to pull in at the first safe and convenient place she could find. When she arrived back at the test centre, I went over to the vehicle to find out that she had failed her test. I checked her driving test report to find one serious fault on her sheet. I then asked her, 'What did the examiner say to you about the serious fault?' She said that the examiner said, 'Why did you stop like you did? You were causing a traffic jam.' She said, 'Because there was an emergency vehicle behind me and my instructor said that I must pull over in a safe and convenient place to let them pass.' The examiner then said, 'Yes, but only if they are displaying their blue flashing lights.'"

One final story: my pupil and I were travelling along a dual carriageway practising overtaking skills. We moved out into the right-hand lane to overtake a slower moving vehicle when we both noticed a white van man flashing his lights at us in our rear view mirrors. I said to the pupil, "Don't get involved in any sort of conflict with them, and don't feel intimidated by their actions. Just stay nice and calm." The white van man continued flashing his lights until we eventually moved back to the left-hand lane after completing our overtaking manoeuvre. It was tempting to use signs that are not in the Highway Code to the person in the white van, but I thought better of it with my pupil sitting next to me.

On glancing over to the white van man as he was passing us, I noticed that he was waving and shouting my name out of his window. "All right, Paul, how you doing?"

It was only then that I realised it was one of my ex-pupils who had recently passed his test and was quite excited of the fact that he was now one of the famous White Van Man Gang.

23

What's That in Your Bag

I picked up a pupil for her driving lesson early one morning from her house when I noticed she had a large bag with her. That normally means they want dropping off somewhere else. As she put the bag on the back seat of the car, I asked her the question, "Do you want dropping of somewhere else or back at home?"

She replied, "Oh, at home, please. I had a sleepover last night at my friend's house and I have just arrived back home this morning." My pupil placed the bag on the back seat before getting into the driving seat.

I still wasn't sure why she brought the bag with her, but she did. Before moving off, I always check the back seat to make sure that nothing can fall off the seat; in her case, I checked to see that her bag was closed and nothing would fall out. Her rather large bag was full to the top, and open, so I said, "I am just going to place your bag on the floor behind your seat to stop anything falling out."

"That's fine."

As I moved her bag on to the floor behind her seat, a silken garment fell out. To me it looked like a silk scarf. I showed her the garment and said, "This item just fell out of your bag. Would you like me to put it back in your bag, or would you like to wear it?"

She looked at me with horror and said, "What are you doing with my knickers?"

"I am so sorry. I thought it was a silk scarf."

"No," she said, "they are my knickers."

Ouch. I didn't know what to say, so I just gave her my apologies again. She actually found it quite amusing, but it made me feel very uncomfortable. Why would you leave your knickers on top of your bag? I am still trying to work that one out.

24

Why Me

Sometimes you wonder what you may have done wrong in your past life to be blessed with such amazing pupils. Most modern cars today are fitted with self-cancelling signals, so that when you steer the wheel back after negotiating a junction, the signal will go off by itself, if it doesn't, then I tell the pupil that they just need to give the indicator a short tap to turn it off. On one occasion after, negotiating a corner, the pupil started to swerve all over the road from right to left.

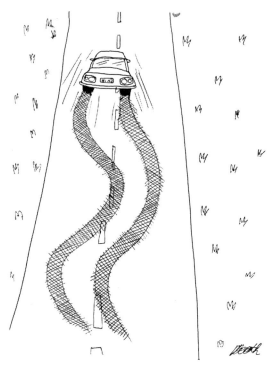

I eventually had to grab the steering wheel and get her to drive a straight line.

I asked her why she was steering so erratically along a straight road, and her reply was "I was trying to get the indicators to self-cancel."

25

Geary Me

There are sometimes when the pupil asks me if their friend or parent or in this case the woman's husband can accompany them in the car. I have no problem with that, and in fact I actually like it so they can see how I teach on the driving lesson. This one day this lady's husband came along, and we were well in to the lesson when we pulled over for a recap of her driving so far. I started by saying that her gear changing had improved to a really good standard compared with last week's lesson, so well done for that. She said she had been practising her gear changing.

"I thought you didn't have a car to practice in," I said.

"No," she said, "I haven't. I practice while I'm in bed."

Still confused, I said, "How do you practice your gears in bed?"

I looked over my shoulder at her husband to see whether he could shed any light on the matter. He just smiled at me like the Cheshire cat. The penny soon dropped as to how this was possible.

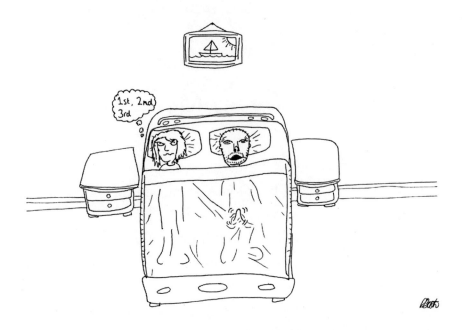

I said, "I am just glad I haven't taught you reverse yet. That could be quite a painful experience for your husband."

26

Risk It for a Biscuit

Having an interest in what pupils have to say is important for a good working relationship. I had just pulled over at the end of my pupil's lesson, and after the recap I inquired, "What will you be doing for the rest of the day?"

He said, "Oh a lot of my family will be coming around, including my grandma, my aunty and uncle, my brother and sister, and we are going to watch the Grand National Horse Race."

I take an interest in horse racing, so I said to him, "I didn't realise you and your family were into betting on horses."

He replied, "We don't bet with a real bookie."

"You mean you don't go in to a betting shop on the high street."

"That's right."

"So what do you do? Do you bet online or something like that?"

"No, nothing like that. My mum goes into town in the morning and buys lots of different types of biscuits, rich tea, digestives, custard creams, and chocolate hob knobs. We then divide half of all the biscuits between us, with us all getting an equal share of rich tea, custard creams, digestives, and chocolate hob knobs. We then decide which horse we think will win, and if you really fancy that horse a lot you place your favourite biscuit or biscuits on that horse. If you don't fancy a horse that much, you put your least favourite biscuit or biscuits on that horse. If you win you get the equivalent in biscuits back."

It sounds a lot of fun. However, I just couldn't see myself getting to excited if my horse was in first place after jumping the last fence knowing I might win two chocolate biscuits.

27

Star Jump Man

As we know hindsight is a wonderful thing, this one morning I would have definitely stayed in bed if I had known what the day had in store for me. My pupil and I were travelling along a busy road, minding our own business enjoying the midday sunshine when a elderly gentleman decided that he would cross the road. At first glance there seemed no danger, until for some unknown reason he started to perform star jumps, waving his arms up and down and jumping sideways like a crab on acid.

We were mesmerised and transfixed by the gentleman's actions. I started to gently brake along with my pupil until we both felt there was no more danger; however, just when we thought that the danger had gone, he decided to cross the road again. This time we did hit him, sending him flying in to the nearby bus shelter. we then watched as he bounced out onto the footpath.

My pupil and I stopped the vehicle, and I went to see if he was all right. He seemed to be stable, so I called emergency services. The operator asked me about the gentleman's condition.

I said, "He seems a little dazed and confused. Wait a minute, he is getting up. No, hold on, he has just fell down again." He was going up and down like a yo-yo. The police arrived to find the gentleman still on the pavement but in a stable condition. The gentleman was well known to them and the ambulance crew. Apparently he is well known for wasting police time by making hoax phone calls; however, this time it was for real.

I think it was quite obvious from what had happened and what the police had to say that the gentleman was a few sandwiches short of a picnic. The pupil, to my amazement, was not shaken up in any way. She was more than willing to drive on to see if we could find anybody else who would like to get run over. We continued the lesson as if nothing had happened.

28

Nowt Stranger than Folk

Years ago, when I was a young lad, if you made mistakes you were thought of as being daft or stupid. If you struggled at school with reading or writing you were thought of as not being very clever. Even the teachers seemed to accept that this was the norm and that some pupils are clever and some are not. It was like, *This is the hand you were dealt—deal with it.*

In today's society we seem to have come a long way with medical science, and if I get a pupil that acts strangely or says peculiar things, who doesn't know left from right, or who goes mental with me, there always seems to be an explanation for their strange behaviour. I wish I could turn the clock back and just say to the pupil that in my professional opinion you are a few shillings short of a pound and that you would be better off using a push bike; unfortunately, I am not allowed to do that.

This one day I asked my pupil to turn the car around in the road, using forward and reverse gears trying not to hit the kerb. The manoeuvre started well; he was controlling his speed nice and slowly and was showing great ability in putting a full left lock on. However, halfway across the road he burst out saying, "Sold to the man at the back with the yellow hat on."

Stunned by this, I said, "Sorry, what did you say."

He then repeated, "Sold to the man at the back with the yellow hat on."

"What is all that about?"

"You said the instruction so quickly it sounded like you were an auctioneer trying to sell something, so the first thing that came to my mind was, 'sold to the man at the back with the yellow hat on'."

I was lost for words, thinking maybe I should pre-warn the examiner so they would know what to expect.

On another occasion with the same pupil, again doing a turn in the road, he began shouting out, "Phil Collins!" for no apparent reason. It was easy for me just to ignore the remark this time and continue with the lesson. I don't think I look or sound like Phil Collins, so I am definitely confused by this one.

My next pupil was a young gentleman who was going for his driving test on the day in question. We arrived at the test centre for his driving test in plenty of time, so we could go through all the procedures of the test just before we went in to the test centre. This covered the checking of the Driving Licence. I explained that the examiner would ask you if you still live at the same address on your Driving Licence. A simple yes is all that is required, and then the examiner would say, Thank you, would you like to lead the way to your car please? On this occasion, the pupil, when asked, said, "Yes" with attitude in his voice. Then, as they were leaving the test centre, the pupil said in a loud voice, "I should know where I live. I have lived there for the last ten years. I do know my own address."

The examiner looked over at me as if to say, *What have you brought me?* I just shook my head in disbelief and waited for him to arrive back. Unfortunately he failed his test due to some silly mistake; however, if there had being a section for flippancy, then he would have failed before even leaving the test centre.

I had another pupil that could not look at one of my diagrams because one of the cars in the diagram looked out of proportion with the rest of the cars. I had to cover the car up with my hand before I could continue with the brief.

There are pupils who can't stand it if someone overtakes them, so they try to chase them down the road at excessive speeds, going mental. "Wait until I pass my test, you moron! Then I will have you, moron!"

One thing I found strange: a pupil was reversing around a corner, getting confused as to which way to steer. Now this is quite a normal thing for a pupil to get confused about and normally quite easy to sort out or so I thought. I said to her, "If you need to go towards the kerb, then you steer left towards the kerb, and if you need to get away from the kerb, you steer right away from the kerb." To me that seemed simple; however, the pupil kept steering the wrong way. I was finding it difficult to understand her logic, until the penny dropped. She was steering from the bottom of the wheel. When she pushed the wheel up from the bottom with her right hand, she thought that she was steering right, and when she steered the wheel up from the bottom with her left hand, she thought she was steering left.

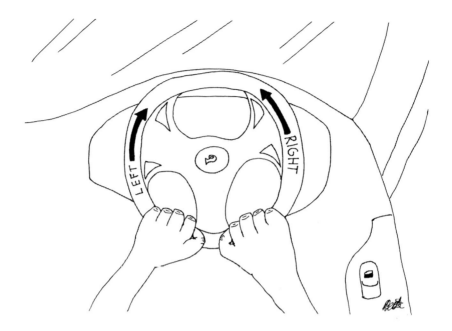

Still confused, so was I, it made no sense to me but made plenty of sense to her; however, I still find it hard to understand the logic behind her thinking. She actually passed her test the second time around with no faults on her test report.

29

Wind Up 1

There are times when a pupil asks you a question that gives you the urge to wind them up. I had just finished the emergency stop brief and was about to explain to my pupil that the signal the examiner would give her for the emergency stop exercise when she stopped me in my tracks and said, "How will I know when to stop?"

I could not resist the temptation to wind her up with a plausible answer. With a serious look on my face, I said, "An examiner will run out into the road from behind that bush, and you must stop quickly, but in control, before hitting him."

There was a deathly silence, and after a few seconds the pupil then said, "Oh my God, you are joking, aren't you?"

"No, I am being serious. That's what they do, but don't worry, you will be fine."

Again there was a deathly silence, until she said, "Oh my God, oh my God, I will hit him, I know I will. I won't be able to do it."

"You will be fine," I said for the second time, trying not to grin.

"How will they know when to run out?"

"Examiners are trained to a high standard, and they do this seven times each day, so they know exactly when to run out. They will see you parked up, and as soon as you move of they will be ready to run out, so you must stay alert."

I also said that the examiner would be wearing a yellow jacket with emergency stop duty on it, as this is part of their ongoing training.

On the day of her test, when she came back, she said, "The examiner didn't run out in front of my car like you said they would."

"Really? What did he do then?"

"He said he would put his hand up and at the same time he would shout stop."

"Really? They must have changed the way they do it. Thanks for that. I will inform my other pupils. I am sure they will be relieved."

30

Double Wammy

I was taking a new pupil from the Carden Park Hotel establishment near to where I live. The pupil was from Northern Ireland and was working has a chef at the hotel to further his career before moving on to better things, like one day running his own restaurant. A few weeks later I took on another pupil from the hotel who was also working there as a chef. My pupils were about three weeks in to their driving lesson and everything seemed to be going well. This one day i arrived at Carden Park to take the pupil from N. Ireland on his driving lesson. When he got in to the car I noticed that he had a gash on the side of his head about 3 inches long. I said to the pupil, "What on earth have you done to your head?"

"I was just about to tell you that I am going to have to cancel my driving lessons, because I am going back to Northern Ireland."

"What does that have do with the gash on your head?"

"I was winding one of my fellow mates up in the kitchen over something and nothing. Unfortunately, he didn't see it that way and threw a tenderising mallet at me, hitting my head with a glancing blow."

I was shocked, and not only that, but disappointed to be losing a pupil. I said, "How come you lost your job. After all, you didn't throw anything at him."

He said, "Because I was the main instigator. The manager had no choice but to fire me."

"Well, what happened to the other person? I hope he got fired as well."

"Oh yes, he got fired has well."

Later on that day I received a phone call from the other chef saying that he would also have to stop having driving lessons because of unforeseen circumstances. I asked him what had caused this sudden change in his circumstances, and he said that he had been fired from his job for throwing a tenderising mallet at another chef because he was winding him up.

I said, "That's terrific. The person you threw the mallet at was also having driving lessons with me, so now I have lost two pupils in a week." At the time I was not amused, it was only later when I was explaining the story to another driving instructor that I saw the funny side of it."

31

Steering Job

Driving in a straight line can be a difficult task for some pupils; however, after a few lessons it usually becomes quite natural. My pupil and I were driving on a long stretch of road with very little in the way of bends when she began to have difficulty keeping a straight line. I asked her if there was any reason why she was drifting all over the road, and her reply was "I am not sure I am just finding it difficult to keep a straight line."

After trying several solutions to the problem, I said that part of the reason she couldn't keep a straight line was that she was sitting on the right-hand side of the vehicle and her perception of her position in the road had also changed. I continued by saying that if one of her parents had been sitting in the passenger seat whilst she was driving they may feel the need to tell her to move over to her left as they would be closer to the kerb This is because they are used to sitting on the right hand side in the driving seat

After the pupil had digested what I had said, she asked, "Is that why some people have the steering wheel on the left hand side of the car, so it will help them keep a straighter line?" I tried to explain about left-hand drive cars but gave up when she couldn't understand about how people drive on the other side of the road in certain countries.

32

Two for Tea

I arrived at my pupil's house for his lesson at about 6:30 pm. The gentleman was an Indian man whose English was limited, but I found him easy enough to understand. Sometimes words that seem logical when you say them can easily be misinterpreted by your pupil in to what you mean, as is the case in this story. I had to talk slowly and clearly for him to understand me, so when he came out of his house and got in to the car, I said, "How are you this evening?"

"I'm okay."

"Have you managed to have your tea before you came out tonight?"

"Yes."

"What did you have for tea?" I asked, thinking he would say something interesting.

"I had coffee."

"Sorry, what did you say?"

"I had coffee, not tea."

The next time he got into the car, I just asked him, "Have you managed to have your evening meal before your driving lesson?"

"Yes, I had curry."

"What about coffee?" I said.

"Oh yes, I had a cup of coffee as well," he said.

33

The Good, the Bad,
and the Sleepy

When pupils pass their test, they can then go on to do their Pass Plus. Pass Plus has been ongoing for many years now, and it includes motorway driving, dual carriageways, rural driving, town or city driving, night driving, and other skills that are more advanced than the normal driving test. You have to have a minimum of six hours tuition taken over a period of time, or like me, I tend to do it as one six-hour lesson with a lunch break in between. I suppose it's kind of an endurance test for your pupil. When the test is completed, the pupil gets a training report that can be exchanged for a certificate through the Driving Standards Agency. This certificate can also be used to get a reduction off their insurance.

THE GOOD: One of my Pass Plus lessons was taking a young gentleman out. I had booked the whole day off from taking learner drivers, so it meant I would have an early finish. I arrived for the gentleman about 9 am., and after explaining all about the format for the day we headed off towards the motorway.

We stopped about a mile from the motorway for a brief, and then we made our way on to the M6. We were heading north when I noticed signs for Blackpool. I said to my pupil, "I haven't been to Blackpool for a long time. I used to go quite regularly with my children."

To which he replied, "I had never been to Blackpool."

"Really? I take it you are not a fan of roller coasters then?"

"Oh yes, I love roller coasters. Just never been."

With in a flash I said, "Do you fancy a day out at Blackpool? I have no more lessons booked for the day. We could go on the pleasure beach, if you like?"

He didn't need asking twice. We drove to Blackpool, taking in motorway driving and then town driving in Blackpool. We had a great time on the pleasure beach in the afternoon and then continued the rest of the Pass Plus on the way home, including his night driving. We arrived home late in the evening, and I can honestly say we both had a great time.

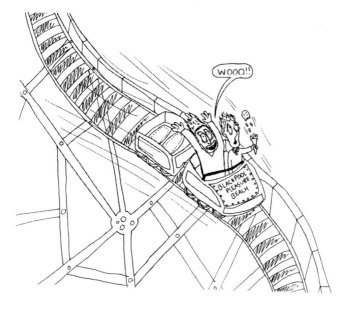

Next time anyone books their Pass Plus with me, it might be worth bringing your passport just in case you fancy a day out in Euro Disney.

THE BAD: I had a call from a lady who had passed her test with me about two months ago, and she was asking me if I could fit her in for her Pass Plus. I replied, "Yes, no problem. When would you like to do it?"

We arranged a date; however, she asked me if she could do it in her own car. I said, "Yes, that's fine, provided that your car is in good working order."

"Yes," she said, "no problem, the car is fine. However, could we go to Bristol on the lesson, because I need to pick up a dog that I have bought?" I was taken by surprise by this, but I agreed, seeing that she was doing it in her own car.

The pupil arrived at my house in her car, as planned. I made my way outside and checked her car over for any defaults like wear and tear on the tyres. The car was road worthy but only just. I got in to find my window wouldn't wind down, the seat wouldn't move properly, and the car itself was a mess inside. We started the journey, and as we moved off I could smell the clutch burning as she applied more gas to get momentum. I said to her, "You are in third gear, and you need to change in to first gear for moving off."

She replied, "It is first gear."

I tried to explain to her that it wasn't, but she wouldn't have any of it. She would argue till the cows came home. She then went in to what she thought was second gear, but it was quite obvious that it was fourth. But she was having none of it. She continued going from third to fourth gear until we reached the motorway about 5 miles away. The motorway journey itself was not without a scare, when a motorway maintenance vehicle pulled out from the hard shoulder without picking up any speed into lane one where we were travelling. We had to swerve quite severely into lane two, almost striking another vehicle, but at least we didn't have to do any gear changing. After leaving the motorway, we continued through Bristol only for the lady to continue her crazy gear changing. By this time I thought we would never get back. The clutch was knackered, and she still continued to argue with me, saying that she had taken it in to a garage to be looked at and they said the gears were fine. At this point I gave up with all her arguing.

We arrived at the kennels and picked up this massive dog, a Japanese Akita, a beautiful dog with a flatulence problem. Remember, my window would not open. On the way back I finally cracked. I said in an angry voice, "Pull over now!" I made her move over so I could sort the out the gears. I got in to the driving seat, and after a while of persevering I managed to sort out the gears. I found first and second and third and fourth, whoopee and then told her to get into the driver's seat. Before I could explain to her where her lost gears were, we were wheel spinning down the road. Power at last, no more burning clutch, saying that, I would be mightily surprised if there was any clutch left to burn out. She said she had been driving her car like this for the last few weeks.

On the way back we had to keep stopping so I could get some fresh air from the dog with the flatulence problem. It smelt liked a vegetarian's fart in her car. The dog would not stop.

It felt as if my military days had returned gas gas gas except I didn't have my gas mask to put on. This was the Pass Plus from hell. We arrived back at my home some two hours later than planned. I was just so glad to get out of her car. Any longer and I think I would have thrown up.

THE SLEEPY: A young but very intelligent pupil who had gained straight A grades was on her Easter break from Cambridge University. I had taught her to drive a few months earlier, and even then we were having some problems, she turned up for her driving test a day late. She told me that she had booked her test for Saturday at 11:21 am. When I picked her up I asked her for her confirmation letter, but she said, "I have left it in my drawer in my room in Cambridge," which was about three hours away from her house. We turned up at the test centre only to find it was closed. She then started to panic and decided to phone her lecturer in Cambridge to get the confirmation letter out of her drawer. When the lecturer phoned back, she said, "Yes, you do have a test booked at 11:21 am., but it was for yesterday Friday, not today."

The pupil was mortified about what her mum would say to her. She said, "My mum will go ballistic with me." I tried to calm her down. As far as I know it was all sorted out.

After she passed her driving test her mum phoned me to see if I could get her booked in for her Pass Plus. With my diary being very busy, I said I could only fit her in at 7:30 am. Her mum agreed and said. "I can't see that being a problem. I will make sure she is up and ready for you, Paul." Unfortunately the pupil had only ever heard of seven thirty in the evening. I turned up for my pupil, and to my amazement she was ready and waiting for me, just as her mum had said. She was looking a little tired, so I thought it best we get started before she fell asleep. We drove off, and as usual I stopped near the motorway for her motorway brief, which lasted about twenty minutes. I am not sure how much of the brief she took on board, but all I can say is that she was looking very tired. We drove down the motorway towards Manchester for a while, when she then said, "How long does the Pass Plus last?"

"Six hours with a half-hour break."

Her eyes nearly popped out of her head. "How long did you say?"

"Six hours."

"Oh my God. There is no way I can drive for that long. I am already tired."

I continued to tell her that her mum was paying me for six hours' tuition so I thought we should do them.

She said, "Can we do just three hours instead?"

"Yes, however, I still require payment for six hours. That is the time I have allocated for today's lesson."

"My mum will go mental with me if I don't do the six hours, and she has to pay for them!"

To which I replied, "Exactly."

"I really can't drive much longer, Paul," she said. "I never get up this early. My mum shouldn't have booked it this early."

I made a suggestion on the basis that I could see that she was too tired to continue driving and would possibly put us both in danger. It was like something from *Only Fools and Horses*, when Del Boy would ask Rodney to help him out of a situation. "Okay, on the one hand, you can't drive much farther, because you are tired, and on the other hand, we can't go back early, because your mum will go berserk if you don't complete the Pass Plus that she is paying for. I've got it," I said. "We will park up when we get to Manchester, and you can go to sleep in my car while I go for a walk around Manchester." It was the only solution to the problem. When we arrived at the car park I said to her, "I am now going for a walk. Make sure you lock the doors of the car and wind your windows up before you get your head down."

I took a walk to Coronation Street to see some of the cast arriving for work. I used to do extra work on the set some years ago, so I was quite familiar with its whereabouts.

I arrived back at my car some three hours later to find her just waking up. She was feeling awake now and ready to go. We continued the Pass Plus, or at least what was left of it, and made our way back home. When we arrived back I had to tell her mum a little porky just to save her daughter's skin. I said to her mum that she had driven well but would need another three hours' tuition to cover other aspects of her driving. Her mum was fine about it and agreed to pay for another three hours' tuition. We then completed the Pass Plus at a later date, and everyone was happy and none the wiser, until now.

34

Wind Up 2

Whilst travelling along a busy road, my pupil drove over a grid, causing the car to jump a little. My pupil asked me what the bump was. To me it was quite obvious, but I could not resist a chance for a wind up. I said, and without much thought for the pupil's feelings. "You have just drove over a cat."

There was a pause of silence from my pupil before she replied, "You are joking, aren't you?"

"No, but don't worry, just carry on driving. You are driving well."

"Oh my God, please tell me I didn't kill a cat."

"Okay, you didn't kill a cat."

"No really, please Paul, did I kill a cat?"

"Yes, you did, but you told me to say you didn't. Just keep driving."

"How can I drive when I have just killed a cat? My mum will go mad with me if I tell her."

"Best not tell her then."

"I need to pull over and stop. I really feel upset. I don't think I can drive any more," she said. We pulled over in a safe place only for my pupil to burst out in tears. I felt that at this point it was too late to tell her the truth.

Guilty as charged, Your Honour.

35

Hook, Line, And Sinker

I was having a conversation with my pupil on the way to Whitchurch, the town where he would be doing his driving test. He was telling me he was in the Air Cadets and was asking me about my military adventures. I was being quite serious about my time in Northern Ireland when he said in a saddened voice, "My Granddad got his tongue shot off in the war."

I was shocked. "Really? That is awful. I am sorry to hear that."

He then said with such a serious look on his face, "No problem, Paul. My Grandad never talks about it."

Revenge will be sweet.

36

What Does This Button Do?

Sometimes you will get pupils that are forever playing with the controls, even when they are driving. This one occasion we were driving along a country road on a hot summer's day. I had my window partially open, with my elbow on the door and my arm in an upwards position. My hand was gripping the top of the roof, and I was just enjoying the fresh air fanning through the window. My pupil at this moment in time decided it would be a good idea to wind my window up without any notification or thought. Before I could blink my fingers were trapped fast.

I yelled out with pain as I managed to open the window from my side. My fingers looked as if they were about to fall off, and I couldn't move them. I spoke to my pupil about the incident, and all she said was "I am really sorry. I just thought I would wind your window up."

I felt like saying a few choice words but thought better of it, as I might regret it later, so I just politely said, "Please don't do it again. I have got my own control for my window."

It is quite amazing. Every time we have a hot day and I have my hand out the window, I actually jump when I see my pupil going to open her window. It has genuinely scared me. I have been scarred for life.

37

Slip Sliding Away

An unusual situation occurred when my pupil and I were approaching a give-way junction in the middle of a residential area. As we approached the junction, I noticed an elderly lady being pushed in a wheelchair on the pavement to my left. As we stopped at the junction, I looked to the left again and saw the elderly lady sliding out of the wheelchair. The person pushing her was a young girl who was not aware of the situation until it was too late. The lady slipped straight out of her wheelchair on to the pavement and was almost in the road under my front wheels. The elderly lady was unaware of the situation she was in, as she was not capable of knowing what was happening due to her illness. The young lady was in distress with what had happened and said to me, "The straps that were holding her in must have come loose."

My pupil and I helped her to get the lady off the road and back in to her wheelchair. It was a difficult task, because every time we tried to get her into her chair, it kept moving back and almost tipped up. I was pulling her up in to the chair with my arms around her chest as my pupil lifted her legs up.

The young lady was doing her best to keep the wheelchair from tipping up, but it was proving to be very difficult. The more we tried to lift the lady in to her chair, the more the chair kept moving. Eventually we got her back in to her chair in some sort of fashion. Without trying to be rude to the lady in the wheelchair, If it had been November 5th, I think people would have been throwing money at us for the best Guy fawkes that is what she looked like once the young lady had strapped her back in to her wheelchair with these big leather straps.

The young lady could not thank us enough for all our help. She was concerned that she would get in to serious trouble if her superiors were to find out. I replied to the young lady, "No problem. It's all in a day's work."

38

Sneezy, Sleepy, Dopey, Doc, Happy, Bashful, Grumpy

I believe that each of these names sums up all or some of my pupils I have taken on driving lessons.

SNEEZY: A pupil of mind was driving along a nice country road minding her own business when she suddenly felt her nose twitch. I could see her drawing breath, ready for the inevitable. Within a split second her nose exploded.

P.W. Wolfendale

She sneezed all over my steering wheel right in front of my eyes. I almost jumped out of my seat with fright with the sudden surprise and loudness of the sneeze. It was hard to believe that someone with just one nose could make that sort of impact like she did. I think the sneeze must have broke the sound barrier at least that's what my ears were telling me. It came out at one hell of a speed all over my steering wheel. I found it very difficult to understand why she couldn't control her sneeze. She said that she was sorry and couldn't help it. We pulled over in a safe place, whereupon I got out of the vehicle and left her to clean up her mess with some wipes I had in my car for these sort of emergencies. It's snot funny when this sort of thing happens.

SLEEPY: Most people can feel tired sometimes on their driving lesson depending on the time of day, how much sleep they had the night before all sorts of things. On driving lessons we generally give a brief of some sort on various topics to do with driving. The brief shouldn't last much more than about seven minutes maximum, because of a pupil's concentration span. I start the brief, and then, with a lot of pupils, some of them would give a yawn or two before the brief is complete. To keep the pupil from yawning, I get my yellow highlighter out and tell them every time they yawn I will make a mark on my diagram to see how many times you yawn. It's amazing how it works. Most of the pupils will do their uppermost not to yawn. However, the award for best yawner goes to a seventeen-year-old lad who plays goalkeeper for a non-league team in the Wirral. I believe I had twenty yawns marked down on my sheet. That works out to about one yawn every twenty seconds.

A yawn to me ranges from any movement of the bottom lip twitching, to the hippo yawn, to a covering of the mouth with their hand. Looking away for more than three seconds is normally a good sign or basically any facial expression that I consider yawn like, and believe me I have seen some in my time. I nick named him the Yawn Meister.

DOPEY: This one has to go to me for filling my car up with unleaded petrol when I have a diesel car. I was very embarrassed with the whole escapade. It was the morning of my pupil's test, everything was running like clockwork as I arrived at my pupils house. We drove towards the test area, and on the way I said to him, "I will need to fill up with some diesel before your test."

Here come the excuses, so laugh if you must. We went to a petrol station that I was unfamiliar with. I got my pupil to pull alongside the petrol pump only to realise that he pump we pulled alongside was all V power fuel, about 10p a litre more. I looked around the station to find that all the other pumps seemed to be V power as well. I went in to the shop and asked the assistant, "Which pump is your regular diesel? I can't seem to find one."

She said, "Pump one by the shop is your regular diesel."

I returned to the car and explained to my pupil which pump we needed to drive to. It was quite awkward to manoeuvre the car, so we ended up with the passenger side right up against the pump. The problem was my petrol cap was on the driver's side. I couldn't see what writing was on the nozzle because we were so close, so I picked up the dark purple nozzle, leaving the green one and one other that had a white label on top of it. I stretched the nozzle over and then checked the price to make sure it matched up to the price of what the diesel should cost.

Bingo, the price matched up to what the diesel should have cost: £1.41 per litre. I filled up with £25 worth of fuel, and after paying for it I left with my pupil. We drove about 200 yards up the road to an area where we could practice the left reverse exercise before the pupil's test. It was only then that I realised something was wrong, when the car started to make a strange noise as if it was about to stall.

For some reason I had this horrible thought that I had put the wrong fuel in my car. I checked the receipt to find, to my horror, that I had put V power unleaded petrol in my tank. I was mortified and could still not believe what I had done. I glared at the receipt once more, hoping that I had misread it, but I hadn't.

I could see my pupil was looking very concerned as we walked back the petrol station to have it out with the attendant.

I spoke to the attendant with anger in my voice, still not understanding how the mistake had happened. I said, "I thought you said that this pump was not V power."

She said, "I said that this was the regular diesel. I didn't say there was no V power fuel here."

I continued to ask questions. "What is the price of your regular diesel?"

"£1.41."

Then I asked her, "What is the price of you V power fuel?"

"£1.41 also."

"Brilliant," I said, "how confusing is that, having them both at the same price?"

The pupil was gutted, to say the least, as I was.

He could not take his test, so his test fee was lost, while I had to get the AA out to pump all the contaminated fuel out of my car. The whole day cost me about £300 I paid for a retest for my pupil, and also I couldn't charge the pupil for the lesson he didn't have. The cost for pumping the fuel out and cleaning the tank was £200, and there was further costs for lessons that I had to cancel that day.

I managed to get a new test for my pupil within two weeks, and I am pleased to say he passed is test with no faults on the driving test report. Alls well that ends well.

DOC: You wouldn't think I could find anything to do with Doc. Well, maybe not Doc, but certainly Doctor. One of my pupil's mum was into herbal remedies, and this one day, when taking her son on a driving lesson, I happened to mention to her that I was a bit off colour. She asked me, "What are your symptoms?"

Just as a Doctor would, I said, "I have a headache, and my head is feeling very cloudy. My throat is a little sore, but apart from that I am feeling fine."

Bad move. She invited me in to her surgery, where I was welcomed by all sorts of home made herbal recipes. It was like entering a witch doctor's pharmacy. Looking at all the potions, she found one that she said would make me feel better.

I said to her, "I will be fine. I will have a paracetamol." she responded by saying "don't be silly, get some of this medicine down you".

She poured this disgusting liquid in to a glass that was the colour of a technicolor yawn. "Down in one," she said, no questions asked. I did as I was told; there was no turning back now. It was rank, absolutely revolting.

"That will make you better," she said with a smile on her face.

I said, "I will be off now. See you next week." I couldn't wait to get out of the house.

I returned the next week for her son's driving lesson, when she asked me, "Are you feeling any better now?"

"My headache and sore throat have now disappeared, but I started to feel really sick after I dropped your son off. I went home and I was sick several times, but I am fine now. Honestly, I couldn't feel any better, so thanks again for your help."

"Any time," she said, "let me know if you ever feel poorly again."

"Yes, no probs," I said. Funny enough, I never did feel poorly again. I would definitely recommend this recipe for your children when they say they are not well and don't want to go to school today. One glass of that and they will never dare say they are not feeling well again.

HAPPY: I think this has to go to a pupil I was taking from Chester. I was taking this seventeen-year-old boy on his driving lesson, and on return from his lesson we stopped outside this house just around the corner from where he lives off the main road. He pointed out that the young girl who lived there with her parents had just won the lottery, and she was now a millionaire. I was gob smacked and said how lucky she was to have won all that money. We both agreed that it would be amazing to win the lottery and only wished it could have been me.

The boy passed his test, and then about a year later I then got a phone call from the same family asking me if I could now take their daughter for driving lessons now that she had reached seventeen. "No problem," I said and arranged her first driving lesson. About two weeks later I picked her up as usual for her driving lesson to find out that her family had also won the lottery that weekend. I thought it was a joke at first, and that I would wake up in a minute to the smell of coffee, but oh no, I wasn't dreaming. I was now sitting next to a young girl whose parents were laughing all the way to the bank.

The irony of this is a week later, she failed to turn up for her driving lesson appointment, so on her next lesson I said to her, "I will have to charge you for missing your appointment."

"Well, I have only got enough money for today's lesson, so I will need to speak to my mum and pay you on my next lesson."

On her next lesson she said, "My mum is only willing to pay for one hour of the two that were booked on the grounds that she felt it was partly your fault for not parking exactly in the same spot that you parked last week."

I did explain to her that I can't always park in the same spot every week, but to no avail. I never did get payment for the one hour I was owed. She went on to pass her test about two months later, and that was that. They say things come in threes, so I am just keeping my fingers crossed it might be me next time.

BASHFUL: I get lots of pupils who are shy, so there is no particular person whom I could talk about. I find that bashful pupils can make you feel uncomfortable. They tend to be silent when you could do with some kind of feedback, and they make you feel that you have done something wrong when all is fine. I feel that I have to be really sensitive and careful not to upset them. One wrong word out of place and you find yourself squirming in your seat, and that makes it difficult to give constructive criticism. I remember one young lad who wouldn't say boo to a goose. I asked him why he had made a certain mistake, and then he burst out in tears and apologised to me.

"I am sorry for being disobedient."

Out came the tissues.

The same can be said for a young girl I was teaching. We stopped at the side of the road for a recap on her driving so far. I said a few words, and that was enough to start her crying.

Most of the pupils that are quite bashful go on to pass their test; however, one or two will tend to walk away from driving until later on in their lives, as they find it difficult to cope with the pressure.

GRUMPY: I have the perfect candidate for this one, a lady in her late years of life decided that she would have a refresher lesson to keep up to date with all the changes that had occurred since she last passed her driving test. I think more people should do this, so I was pleased that she was taking a refresher lesson.

I arrived on time for her first lesson but could not find her house. I phoned her from my car, and when she answered the phone I said that I couldn't find her house. She tried to explain to me where it was, but then she said in a very grumpy voice, "It would be a lot easier if I walked around the corner to where you are parked. Don't move."

I didn't dare. Within a minute, this grumpy elderly lady approached my car, reminding me of a farmer with her baggy trousers tucked in to her wellies and wearing a woollen cardigan. She got into the passenger side, where I explained the structure of the lesson. I also showed respect to her by saying, "Would you like me to call you by your first name?"

"No," she said, "I would prefer to be called Mrs Smith, please."

"Okay then, would you like to get in to driver's seat, Mrs Smith, and I will get into the passenger seat."

We started the lesson driving on quiet roads, then moved into a little more traffic. The two-hour lesson went quite well, to be honest, even though she made me feel uncomfortable with her presence. She agreed that she would like to book another lesson with me, so the following week I turned up as normal.

"Hello, Mrs Smith," I said. There was no response from her, as she just got in to the car as if she didn't need to be polite to me because she was paying me for my time.

We drove off to the city to try her hand in busy traffic and to get her more up to date with all the different road layouts. Whilst negotiating a busy city roundabout she suddenly changed lanes from the centre to the right lane without any thought for traffic that might have been in the right-hand lane. Because of the sudden change in direction and the fact that she never checked her off side mirror, I grabbed the steering wheel to correct her line. She was startled by my intervention and made it quite clear to me that she was not happy with the fact that I had done this. I had to suffer her aggressive grumpy voice all the way back to her house. When we arrived back we had a recap, and to my amazement she wanted to book another lesson. I was thinking, *Why? You hate me. Why me? What have I done to deserve this?*

I turned up for her next lesson, and things were not quite as they should have been. I parked on her drive and was just about to get out when she came marching out of her house

"Stay where you are."

"Yes, sir," I said. "Whatever you say."

She then got into the passenger side and told me not to turn the engine on. "I need to discuss the matter of you grabbing the steering wheel last week," she said. "I have spoken to several people, including a policeman, and I feel that what you did was wrong."

I think she must have spent all week phoning people to get enough ammunition to shoot me with. She laid in to me big time, not even pausing for breath. All this took about forty-five minutes before she calmed down. I said, "Shall we do some driving now?" and her reply was, "I need to put the chickens away first before opening the gates." She got out of the car to put the chickens away; however, as soon as the chickens saw her approaching them, they knew that that was the signal to put themselves in their coops in a kind off military fashion. "Left right left right left right left." I think they knew better than to argue with Mrs Grumpy.

She then invited me in to her garden, where we spent the next half an hour walking around her garden. She was trying to explain to me about the leaves on the ground and the purpose of them, about the fish in her pond, and all the different tree names in her garden. With thirty minutes of the lesson left she decided it would be pointless to go driving now.

"Why don't we go and have a nice cup of tea."

I just sat and listened to her telling me all about her family tree, until it was time to leave. You would not believe what she said before I left. "Can I book another lesson?"

I went white with fear. "Are you sure you would like another lesson?"

"Yes," she said.

I booked her in on my diary and left her house without once looking back. I was trying to put next week's lesson with her out of my mind; otherwise, it would have ruined my whole week. I received a phone call from her about two days later, just before

I was due to take her out again. "I have decided not to have any more lessons with you," she said. "I still feel that when you grabbed the steering wheel you were wrong in your actions."

"That's absolutely fine," I said, "You know what I think? You might be right. In fact, yes, you are right. Enjoy your day." Then I hung up the phone with a sigh of relief on my face. Bye bye, Mrs Grumpy.

39

A What Car?

My pupil whose name was Jess was telling me that she might be getting a car to practice in soon. I replied, "That would be nice. It should help you to improve your driving."

Jess then said, "My mum is buying me a knicker car."

WHAT IS THAT!

I thought, *What the hell is a knicker car?*

"Pardon me for sounding a bit dumb," I said, "but what is a knicker car?"

Jess then repeated, "No, my mum is buying me a knicker car."

"I heard what you said, but what is a knicker car?"

"No," Jess said, her voice getting louder all the time, "my mum is going to buy Me and Nick a car."

"Okay," I said, "now I understand." Nick was the name of her husband. I just had to laugh, as I had vision of a car full of knickers.

40

Wind Up 3

I had just been to the pet shop to buy some locusts for my son's lizard before picking my pupil up. The pupil was a Chinese man who went by the name of Alan. On picking him up, he noticed the locusts in the back seat of the car. Alan said, "What are those creatures on the back seat?"

"Locusts, why?"

"What you have locust for?"

"They are for my tea."

"You eat them for tea?"

"Yes, they taste lovely."

I didn't think Alan believed me, until he said, "How you cook 'em?"

"I put them in the frying pan with some garlic butter until they are nice and brown."

"How you get 'em in pot?"

I was starting to grin a bit now but still managed to keep a straight face. "You have to take the lid off the pan and then empty the locusts into the pan as quick as possible. You then put the lid back on to the pan before they jump out. I will bring you some on your next lesson."

He declined. "No, please, I not want any locust."

41

Reasons to Be Cheerful

When you start the first driving lesson with a new pupil you can normally tell if they are going to be hard work, and if you are not sure on the first lesson if they are going to be hard work, then you would definitely know by the second lesson. Here is a list of my reasons to be cheerful.

- You know it is going to be hard work when the pupil holds the steering wheel so tight it loses its shape.

- You know it is going to be hard work when your pupil brakes with their left foot while their right foot is on the accelerator.

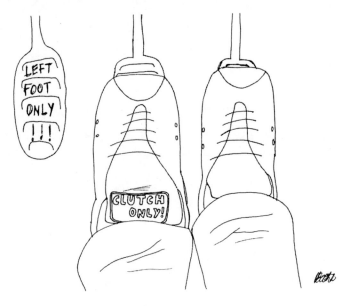

- You know it is going to be hard work when your pupil calls the gear lever the clutch.

- You know it is going to be hard work when your pupil stays silent throughout the whole lesson.

- You know it is going to be hard work when you keep looking at your watch to see how much time there is left on the lesson.

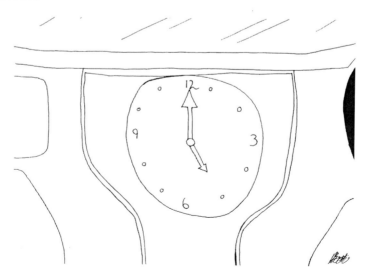

- You know it is going to be hard work when they ask you, "Which side of the road do I drive on?"

- You know it is going to be hard work when they call the indicators the flickers.

- You know it is going to be hard work when you find yourself with your foot permanently on the dual-control brake.

- You know it is going to be hard work when your pupil asks you what the reverse gear is for.

- You know it is going to be hard work when you ask your pupil to change gear and they try to apply the hand brake.

- You know it is going to be hard work when you turn up for your pupil at 6 pm. for their driving lesson and they are still hung over from the night before.

42

Parents Know Best

There are times when your pupil asks you, "Do you think it would be all right for me to go driving with my parents once I get a little more driving experience with you?"

I explain to the pupil, "Yes, I would certainly recommend it; however, if you feel that your relationship with your parent becomes a little hostile when you are driving, then maybe it would better not to drive with them. First, you must remember that they don't have dual controls, so they may become a little more verbal with their instructions, and also the instruction they give you may not necessarily be as clear as the ones I would give you.

I was talking to one of my pupils about her adventures with her parents. She told me that she was driving with her father the other night when her father told her to slow the car down. "I told him I was not exceeding the speed limit and that the speed limit on this road was 60 mph," she said. "My father was having none of it, and he insisted that the speed limit was 40 mph. I told him that I had driven along this road several times with my driving instructor and he should know what the speed limit was. At this point my father then threw a dickey fit and said, 'If you don't stop the car immediately you will be in big trouble, not trouble but big trouble.' I then said, 'There is nowhere to stop. You will have to wait until I can find a suitable place.' My father wasn't willing to wait until I could find a safe place, so without any word or warning he snatched the handbrake on, and the back of the car spun around, causing the back of my car to hit the side of a small bridge we were driving over.

The back of the car was all smashed in. My father went loopy with me, even though it was not my fault. He then decided that he would drive the car back home himself. We argued all the way back home and came to the conclusion that it would be best to leave it to the driving instructor from now on."

In another story, after taking a young girl for her first driving lesson, she said, "My parents only want me to have about ten hours' tuition initially and then they will be taking me out driving."

I told the girl, "It is a good idea for them to take you out driving; however, I would still recommend that you keep having driving lessons in between driving with your parents. That way you won't get into too many bad habits."

On her next lesson she said, "I have spoken to my parents about what you said, but they are still adamant that I have no more than ten hours' driving tuition and they will continue taking me out driving. They want me to start up with you again when I have had more experience on the roads with them." I was in no position to argue, even though I knew it was not the best way forward. After the completion of her ten hours she stopped driving with me and went driving with her parents, as advised.

One week later I received a phone call from her mum asking me if could I fit her daughter in for some more driving lessons ASAP. I said, "Of course. I thought you were going to leave it for a while until she became more experienced on the roads."

"We were," she said, "however, my daughter and I have had a crash on a roundabout, and the car is a write-off."

I was shocked to hear the news and asked if they were all okay. "Yes," she said, "it could have been worse. She just pulled out on to the roundabout without checking to the right and we got splattered.

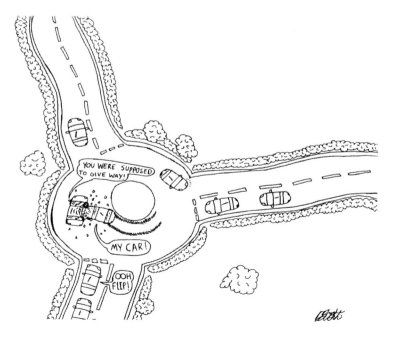

It shook us both up, but at least we were not seriously hurt."

As a driving instructor I find it difficult to understand Why parents don't listen to what we say. In the end the decision to stop having driving lessons after the first ten hours proved to be very costly. The young girl went on to pass the test on her first attempt

All these stories seem to be about young girls, and this one is no different. I was taking this young girl driving, and she was very close to taking her driving test. On her driving lesson she said to me, "My mum has been telling me to approach roundabouts in a complete different way to what you have taught me."

I told her, "Don't worry. Just go back to the way I have taught you when you are with me, and when you are with your mum, it's best you do what your mum says."

At the end of the lesson my pupil asked me, "Would it be possible for you to speak to my mum about the way she expects me to approach roundabouts?"

I felt that it would have been wrong for me not to speak to her mum in the interest of my pupil, so I agreed. At the end of the lesson I followed my pupil into her house and upon meeting her mum I said, "Your daughter would like me to have a word with you about the way she is approaching roundabouts with you."

Before I could explain to her what she should be doing her daughter, her mum kicked off and said, "Fine, I will let her crash then. She can kill us both". I tried to explain to her that she did not understand what I meant. She was having none have it; she then said she was not going to pay for any more driving lessons for her daughter.

I said to her, "It's probably best I left now. I will leave it to you to sort the matter out with your daughter."

I received I phone call from her daughter the next day saying, "My mum will not change her mind, and I am not allowed to have any more driving lessons." With her test being in two weeks' time, she decided to meet me without her mum's permission. She said she wanted to carry on with some more driving lessons. "I have enough money of my own to pay for more lessons." We continued with her lessons without her mum knowing anything about them. I would pick her up after school and then drop her off around the corner from her house. Two weeks later she took her driving test and passed on her first attempt. I was so pleased that she had passed her driving test, no thanks to her mum. To this day I don't know what she said to her mum when she arrived home on that day; I would have loved to have been a fly on the wall when she walked into her house and told her mum that she had passed her driving test.

43

Licence to Thrill

A pupil of mine was taking her driving test. The girl in question was a bit of a rebel to say the least. Very often she would tell me tales about how she use to skive off sixth form college, smoke behind her parents' back, get drunk with her mates I think you get the picture. I enjoyed taking her on her driving lessons, as there was never a dull moment. I was always intrigued to hear what she had to say on her lesson. On the day of her test I picked her up one hour before her test and went through the normal routine of practising her manoeuvres before arriving at the test centre.

On arrival we went into the test centre, and within a few minutes the examiner came out to greet my pupil and take her on her driving test. I waited about thirty minutes for her to come back off her test. Just as I was looking out of the test centre window I saw her arriving back, whereupon I noticed that she had not passed her driving test. I went over to her once the examiner had got out of the car and tried to console her. She was a little upset, but after a few verbal s about what she thought of the examiner I drove her back home. We had a chat about what we were going to do next now that she had failed her test, and she said she would get it booked ASAP. About an hour later I went back to my driving school's office for a well-earned break and to have a cup of tea. As I walked through the door, my branch manager shouted, "Paul, I have just received a phone call from your pupil's mum who took her test today. She would like to thank you for getting her through her driving test."

I replied, "Well that is very nice of her; however, my pupil didn't pass her test today she failed."

The branch manager then said, "No, you have got it wrong. She passed her test."

"No, she didn't pass her test. She failed her test."

The branch manager was now looking confused and thought that I was just joking. I looked my branch manager in the eyes, got within about 6in of her face and said in a slow a calm voice watch my lips.I am not joking, she really did fail her driving test.

The branch manager was mortified and couldn't believe what I was telling her. She thought it best to phone the pupil's house to explain to her mum that her daughter had not passed her test today. The branch manager phoned her house.

"Hello, this is the branch manager from the driving school," she said. "Who am I speaking to please?"

"Oh right," said a voice on the other end of the phone. "Can I first thank you for getting my sister through her test? I am her older brother."

The branch manager said, "I'm afraid I have some bad news for you. Your sister didn't pass her driving test today. She failed her driving test."

Her brother then said, "No, she definitely passed her test today. I have spoken to her."

The branch manager had to repeat, "I have spoken to your sister's driving instructor, and he has assured me that she has failed her driving test."

Her brother didn't know what to say. "I can't believe what she has done," he said. "She has done some really bad things in her time but nothing as bad as this. She has taken her car and driven it to college, having me and her mum believe that she had passed her test. Her mum will go ballistic with her when she catches up with her."

I am not sure what went on when her mum finally caught up with her, but after about a month she came back to me for some more driving lessons and passed her test on her second attempt.

44

Record Breakers

I have put together an interesting collection of true facts that I have called the 'record breakers'. These facts are all taken from pupils I have taught to drive.

MOST TESTS TAKEN

The most tests taken by one of my pupils is ten, by a seventeen-year-old girl who had taken three driving tests before she even came to me. She had three more driving tests with me before I went away for two-week holiday. I came back from my holidays to find out she had taken another driving test with another driving instructor from the same driving school I worked for and had failed for a seventh time. She then came back to me and failed another two driving tests. I spoke to her mum shortly after her ninth test, and her mum said to me that her daughter was going to have a break from driving for a while. "I took her out the other day, and I had to yell at her to stop has she tried to go through a red traffic light."

A year later I took on her brother, who managed to pass his driving test the first time. He said to me that his sister had finally passed her driving test with another driving school on her tenth attempt.

MOST MAJOR FAULTS

The most major faults I have had on a driving test report was seven. I am not proud of this, as it's a record any driving instructor would be ashamed of. It was the pupils fourth driving test. On previous tests he had received three majors on one of his tests, two majors on another test, and just one on his last driving test. I was shocked to say the least. I spoke to him about it and asked him if he could explain what had gone wrong.

"I just lost it in the first two minutes of my test and then drove with a careless attitude after that."

I am at this moment waiting for him to book his fifth driving test.

MOST MINOR FAULTS, OLD-STYLE TEST

Before the driving test was changed some years ago, you could get as many minor driving faults has the examiner gave you without failing your test. Today as it stands you can only get up to fifteen minor driving faults; anything more than that and you will fail your test. The record for the most minor driving faults is held by my cousin. She managed to accumulate twenty two. With the fact that she avoided getting any major faults the result of the test was a pass. The old-style driving test was only about twenty-five minutes long, so that works out almost one fault for every minute of her test.

MOST MINOR FAULTS, NEW-STYLE TEST, WITHOUT ANY MAJOR FAULTS

To pass your driving test, the new-style test requires you to get no more than fifteen minor driving faults and no major faults. One day I was talking to the examiner after he had taken one of my pupils on his driving test. We were talking about the amount of minor faults that pupils accumulate on their test, and I was surprised when he mentioned that a lot of pupils get quite a few minor faults on their test report, and with some going well over the fifteen minor driving faults that they are permitted. I then mentioned that I had never had a pupil who had failed with only minor faults and no majors on their driving test report. Bad move by me. The next week I had a driving test that was conducted by the examiner in question, and, you guessed it, he failed my pupil with sixteen minor driving faults and no majors.

LEAST DRIVING FAULTS

This is one I don't mind talking about. It is very rare that a pupil will come back from their driving test without any faults at all. I am pleased to say I have had eight clean sheets in my twenty years has a driving instructor. On one occasion a young girl I was taking failed her first driving test with just one major fault and no minor faults on her driving test report. This is also almost unheard of; however, on her second test she did even better and got no faults at all on her test report. Quite amazing to get no minor faults at all on her two driving tests. The examiner spoke to me after the driving test and said, "I am pleased to say she has no faults at all on the driving test report."

I said to the examiner, "She only got one major on her last test."

He said, "It makes me feel better to know that another examiner also saw that her driving is at a very high standard and that I didn't miss anything."

LONGEST TIME WITH ONE PUPIL

The longest time I have had a pupil is about eight years. The pupil started with me when she was seventeen, and the last time

I saw her was when she was twenty-five. Her brother had passed his driving test in three months during the time she was having driving lessons with me. She started off having two-hour lessons for the first few months and then cut them down to one-hour lessons. There were breaks in her driving for holidays, exams, and generally taking time out to get her thoughts together. I kept thinking she would not come back; however, she never failed to let me down, and just when I though the coast was clear she would phone me up again to get booked in for more driving lessons. I don't care to guess how many driving lessons she took in her eight years with me it was obviously a lot. I do feel that she would eventually have taken her driving test, but she never even took her theory test in all the time she was with me. That meant she could not book her driving test, as you need to pass your theory test before you can book a driving test. It has been years since I last heard from her. I honestly believe that one day I will be sitting at home and the phone will suddenly ring, and it will be my blast from the past.

SHORTEST TIME WITH ONE PUPIL

My shortest time with a pupil is one week. The lady in question started her lessons on a Saturday and passed her driving test the following Friday, on her first attempt. The lady needed to pass her test quickly, so she was booked in for six hours a day three hours in the morning and then three hours in the afternoon after having lunch. There was no theory test to be taken at this time; this came in years later, so we could book her test straight away.

LEAST AMOUNT OF HOURS TAKEN

I had a young man who had never driven before but was an expert in the art of driving go-kart s. He had never driven on the main roads before, and I taught him everything I could in six hours flat. He then went away and practised the skills with his dad before I took him for his test. After about three weeks he passed his driving test on his first attempt, however. I do think it was down to a certain amount of luck. Sometimes, it is how you perform on the day.

LONGEST DISTANCE TRAVELLED BY PUPIL

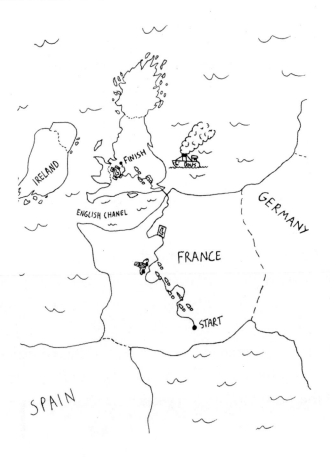

There are some occasions when pupils will travel quite a long distance to get the right instructor in the right area, or to do an intensive course. I had a pupil that came all the way from France. He had an English girlfriend whom he had met when she was working in France as part of her French course. He himself had spent over six months in England studying, which was enough time to allow him to take his driving test in England (you must have resided for at least 165 days in this country over the previous twelve months to be allowed to take your driving test in England). He was looking for an instructor in the Northwest area and got my details from my website. He decided it would work out a lot cheaper even after flying over to take his test in England. In his country, you have to have a minimum set of hours with a driving instructor, and the lessons were very expensive.

He flew over with his girlfriend and had about ten hours with me over three days. His girlfriend sat in on the lessons to help with the language barrier, and she also sat in on his test as an interpreter. Unfortunately he didn't pass his test; he got one major fault, which was enough to fail him. He turned out of a junction and got confused with which side of the road to drive on, with the fact that in his country they drive on the other side of the road

He flew back to France the same day and then came back again two more times, finally passing his test on the third occasion.

LONGEST DISTANCE TRAVELLED BY ME

When I was working for a driving company they asked me if I could go to Aberystwyth in Mid Wales to do a one-hour driving lesson with a gentleman from the post office. The driving school I was with had a contract with the post office to check the standard of their new drivers. There was no instructor in the Mid Wales area to take him, so I was asked if it was close enough for me to take the lesson. I checked my sat-nav to find the distance was over 100 miles, 200 miles round trip. I said the only way I would do the one-hour lesson was if you paid me for five hours four hours travelling time and the one-hour lesson. To my amazement the school agreed to pay what I had asked. A great day was had by all.

OLDEST PERSON I TAUGHT TO DRIVE

The oldest person I ever taught to drive was a lady of sixty-six years of age. She said she was having a new lease of life and wanted to learn to drive. The lady did exceptionally well on her driving lessons, although I had to take the lessons at a rather sedate pace. She passed her test on her first attempt, and she was so pleased she turned to me and said, "This one is for all the senior citizens out there."

YOUNGEST PERSON I TAUGHT TO DRIVE

If you have a disability it is possible with the permission of the DSA to start driving at the age of sixteen. This allows more time for them to develop ones skills. I took a young lad who started driving when he was just sixteen, and within a few months he passed his driving test on the first attempt, at the young age of sixteen and a few months.

TALLEST PERSON

My tallest person was a young boy who was 6 feet, 8 inches tall, who always needed to push his seat back to its fullest. I think I know where the name back-seat driver came from now. Every time I looked across to speak to him it was like checking my blind spot over my right shoulder.

SMALLEST PERSON

My smallest person was a young girl who measured just 4 feet, 8 inches. She used to bring two cushions with her to give her the height she needed, and even then she could just about see over the steering wheel.

LARGEST FEET

This record goes to a seventeen-year-old boy with size 15 feet. He could cover two pedals with one foot. It was difficult for him to adapt, but adapt he did.

MOST CATS KILLED IN ONE DAY

Two cats not proud of it one in the morning and one in the evening.

45

Wind Up 4

I was talking to my pupil about independent driving whilst we were parked up at the side of the road

"On the independent part of your test, the examiner will pull you over in a safe place and explain to you what they want you to do. They will ask you to follow a series of directions, like, 'Follow all signs A41 to Chester.'"

My pupil said, "How does that work?"

"The examiner will get out of the car and expect you to follow all signs A41 Chester and then make your way back to this location, where the examiner will be waiting for you to return."

"Oh my God," said my pupil, "what happens if I crash?"

"You will fail your test, and the examiner will have to walk back to the test centre."

She then said, "What if I get lost? I am crap with directions."

"You will have about five minutes to get back to this location before your time is up. If you don't make it back within the five minutes, you will fail your driving test."

I have since told her the truth, but it was a great wind up at the time.

46

Got cha

As driving instructors, we try to where possible to drive within the law. If you don't, I can guarantee that there will always be smart arses out there on the roads trying to judge you. On this one occasion I was approaching a set of traffic lights with lots of cars in front and behind me. The road was a single carriageway with a speed limit of 60 mph; however, the road branched into two lanes on approach to the lights to help with the filtering of traffic. I was checking my rear-view mirror and noticed a police motorbike rider about three cars back looking very keen. As I got closer to the lights, which were on green, I was aware that the lights might suddenly change colour. Right on cue, the lights changed to amber. I braked immediately and came to a smooth and controlled stop. The lady behind me, who was quite obviously not checking her mirror, decided to manoeuvre around me into the right-hand lane. There was no way she was going to stop because of a silly learner driver playing by the rules, so she accelerated towards the traffic lights at some speed. They were now turning to red, and she drove straight through the lights without any thought for anyone else on the road.

I checked my rear-view mirror again to see the policeman on his motorbike opening up his throttle. He came flashing past me with his blue flashing lights on and was right on her tail within seconds. He pulled her over into the nearby lay by. As I drove past, the last of the incident I saw was the policeman getting is book out to issue her a ticket.

I think we have all at some time come across irresponsible drivers, but we never get to see them getting caught. It's a great feeling of satisfaction when it happens in front of your eyes.

47

Taxi

There are times when you feel as if you are being used as a taxi, with pupils wanting to stop off at certain places for one reason or another, and there are some pupils that really do use you as a taxi. I remember three occasions in particular.

I

A young girl who was into skiing and wanted to know if I could take her to Rhyl on her driving lesson to see the new ski slope they had built there. I said I could, but we would never get there in a two-hour lesson that she had booked

"Could I book a four-hour lesson then, so we can go?" I agreed, and we had a lovely day out in Rhyl.

TAXI We spent about five minutes looking at the new ski slope before we returned. I think it would have been cheaper for her to have got a taxi.

II

I was picking up this French lady for her driving lesson, and upon arrival she invited me in to her house.

"Just come in for a few minutes, Paul. I have something to ask you." She then asked me if I would do her a favour and drive her to Crewe, my local town. She continued by saying she wanted to pawn her ring her German husband had bought for her. She had had an argument with him, and he would not give her any money even though he was very rich. I was surprised by her request and said, "Are you sure you don't want to drive?"

"Definitely not," she said. "I am not in the mood for driving."

"Okay," I said, "no problem."

We set off to Crewe, and as planned she pawned her ring.

TAXI We then went to a local bar and had a couple of non-alcoholic drinks and a bite to eat. The final leg of the journey was to pick her little girl up from her primary school, and then take them both home. By the way, she passed her test on her first attempt, and even then her arrogant husband (who was still complaining about the amount of hours it had taken his wife to pass her test) said, "She should have passed first time with the amount of hours she has had." I felt like saying, just because we won the World Cup in 1966, you have never forgiven us. The ball was over the line accept it and get on with your life.

III

This story involves two Asian pupils. One of them had already passed his test with me, and the other one was still having driving lessons. I had a phone call from the one who had already passed his test asking me whether i would be able to take him and his mate, the one I was still teaching to drive, in addition their respective girlfriends to Alton Towers for the day and then to Manchester in the evening. I said, "Yes, but it will cost you." Money was no object to the two young lads, so I picked them up early one morning and drove them and their girlfriends to Alton Towers. I returned to my local area to take more of my pupils on driving lessons before returning back to Alton towers at about 5 pm. to pick them up and take them to Manchester.

We arrived at Manchester and headed to the famous curry mile for their evening meal.

On arrival at one of the Indian restaurants, they kindly paid for me to have a meal; however, I had to sit on my own while they enjoyed the company of their girlfriends. I felt like Billy No Mates. Not a problem, I thought, at least I am getting paid for it. To be honest, I enjoyed the day and would probably do it again if asked.

48

Turn the Radio On

One of my young Asian pupils decided that it would be a good idea to have the radio on whilst on his driving lesson. He said to me, "Would there be any chance I could listen to some music?"

"I don't mind if you have it on quiet and it doesn't disturb your driving," I said.

He agreed to my demands, so I turned the radio on for him.

"Is there was any particular radio station you would like to listen to?" I asked.

"I have a CD in my pocket that I have brought just in case I was allowed."

I put the CD on for him, and it was some of the worst music I have ever listened to. It was some sort of Asian music that had lots of noisy beats to it.

I kept my patience throughout the short time it was on; however, it wasn't long before I knew he was taking the piss. From lesson to lesson I allowed him to have the same CD on, which I was now getting peed of with. There was worse to come, because he now wanted to play his music louder and louder; every time I turned it down he kept gradually turning it up, until it was at a level that was bursting my eardrums. We were now at loggerheads; however, he thought it was funny. He couldn't understand that it was now driving me mad and that he was not learning a great deal from his driving lesson. I should have told him to sling his hook, but business is business, and he was a paying customer if he wanted to waste his money, then that was his choice.

On this one lesson he said to me, "Could I be dropped off at the mosque for prayer?"

I said, "What was that you said? I can't hear you for the music."

"Could I be dropped off at the mosque for prayer?"

"You have a wasp in your hair? Quick, open the window and let it out."

He decided to turn the music down and explain to me what he had said. "I would like to be dropped off at the mosque please, if that is okay?"

As we got closer to the mosque, I noticed he had started to turn the music down a few decibels, so I said to him, "Why are you turning the music down? You still have one minute of your driving lesson left." He replied that he was not allowed to have the music on outside the mosque. "Oh, is that so?" I said as I turned the music up full blast. He was now getting some of his own medicine back. I had never seen an Asian man go snow white, before but he did. He was panic stricken as we pulled up alongside the mosque, begging for me to turn the music down.

"Please, Paul, turn the music down or I will be in big trouble".

It was a great feeling seeing him squirm. I said to him, "Now you know what it feels like when I want you to turn the music down."

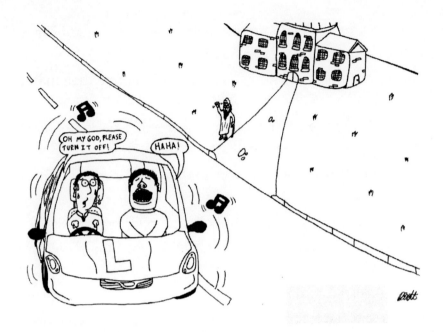

He continued his lessons and passed on his first attempt. We never did have that dreadful music on again.

49

Never Look a Gift Horse in the Mouth

When a pupil passes their test you will find that some of them will buy you a gift of some kind to show their appreciation. As driving instructors we don't expect any sort of gift, so when it happens, it is usually a nice surprise. In the past I have been given money, bottles of wine, whiskey, champagne, pens, a photo frame, vouchers, and even a couple of books full of autographs, as the pupil knew that I collected them. This one day after my pupil had passed her test I arrived back at her house to be greeted by her mum, who thanked me for all the work I had put in, getting her daughter through her driving test on her first attempt. She said, "Just wait there a minute, Paul. I have something for you." I hadn't a clue what my pupil's mum was going to bring me, and after receiving her kind gift I wouldn't have guessed it in a month of Sundays. She brought me half a dozen eggs

"Wow," I said, "thank you kindly."

She then said, "It is a tradition passed down through my family. My mother gave my driving instructor six eggs when I passed my test, and I am doing the same."

"Well, I shall look forward to eating them," I said. "Thank you again."

After all the thank yous had taken place, she then said, "I shall look forward to seeing you in about two years' time, when my son will be seventeen."

"Look forward to it," I said. "See you in two years." Then I left.

Two years later I got another six eggs when her son passed his driving test, and then another six eggs after her son completed his Pass Plus with me. I would like to thank you again for providing me with an egg-straordinary story for my book.

50

Timing Is Everything

Two interesting stories involving timing.

As an ex-military man, timing is very important to me. I never turn up late without good reason, and I would always let my pupils know if I am running late because of traffic or some other cause. It was the day of my pupil's test, I had just finished my first lesson of the day, and I decided to pull over at the side of the road and have a short break since I had some spare time on my hands. Within five minutes of parking up I received a phone call from my pupil.

"What time are you picking him up for my test, Paul?" he said.

"I will be leaving shortly and will be with you at a quarter to eleven."

"It is already a quarter to eleven."

"No, it's not. It's a quarter to ten." It was only then that I realised what I had done. I was working on a twenty-four-hour clock system like they do in the army, so when I saw 1045 on my watch, I was thinking that it was a quarter to ten. I got totally confused with the number ten. I couldn't believe what I had done.

I tried not to sound panicked when I reassured my pupil in a nice, calm voice that I would be with him within three zero minutes, I think that is 30 minutes non-military time. I raced as quick has possible to my pupil, trying to keep within the speed limit. I arrived at his school with only fifteen minutes to spare before his test. With the test centre still about twenty minutes away, I decided to phone and explain my predicament to them. On picking up the phone the examiner said, "I will allow you five minutes grace, and if you arrive any later than the five minutes the test will not take place." I said to my pupil that it would be best if I drove to the test centre because we needed to get there in quick time. We arrived after the five minutes' grace we were told we could have, and we legged it into the test centre. We rang the bell on the examiner's door, and as he opened it we held our breath. He said, "One more minute later and the test would have not taken place." After checking my pupil's documents, he said, "Would you lead the way to your car please?"

My pupil then asked the examiner, "Would it be all right for my instructor accompany me on my driving test?"

"Yes, that would be fine."

I got into the back of the car and waited for my pupil to get in along with the examiner. I never really gave it a thought that my pupil had not driven the car at all today, so his seat and mirrors were not correctly adjusted. He turned the engine on only for the radio to come on playing loud music.

The examiner didn't look too impressed as my pupil fumbled to turn it off. The pupil, now under pressure, drove off and just tried to do the best he could. I was still feeling guilty sitting in the back of the car and felt that if he failed his test then I would have to take responsibility for that and reimburse him for the lesson and the driving test.

We got back to the test centre, whereupon the examiner said, "Would you turn off the engine please." My heart was going ten to the dozen. "I am pleased to say you have passed," said the examiner. "You have several minor driving faults but no major faults."

After all the paperwork had been filled the examiner left the vehicle and I got into the front seat and checked the driving test report to see what faults he had committed. He had got the maximum you are allowed before it is classified as a fail fifteen minors. In my heart of hearts, I really thought it was just going to be one of those days. I feel that the Good Lord was looking down on us that day.

The next tale happened because the clocks go forward in the spring. I had a lesson booked with a young lady at 11:30 am on a sunny Sunday morning. I arrived at her lovely country house to the sound of silence. Within a few minutes, the pupil's mum came out of her front door wearing her dressing gown. I was thinking to myself, it's a bit late in the day to be wearing a dressing gown, but it was Sunday morning after all.

"Hi, Paul," she said. "You are a bit early. My daughter is just getting out of bed."

"No probs," I said, "it's only just 11:30."

Her mum said, "No, it's 10:30," as she looked at her watch. When I explained to her about the clocks being put forward one hour there was one almighty panic. Everyone in the house hold seemed to be affected by the fact they had forgotten to put their clocks forward. I could hear my pupil shouting and screaming from the top of her voice, and then I heard her other sister shouting, "I should have been at work at eleven. Oh my God". She worked at her local restaurant, and they were expecting a lot of people in for lunch. Her mum was also in distress because she and her husband were due to go to church for 10:30. It was like a scene from a sitcom they were all running around like headless chickens, all in different directions. I decided it would be better if I just waited in my car until everybody had calmed down. About fifteen minutes later my pupil eventually came out of her house with a piece of toast in one hand, my money for the lesson in the other, a bag over her shoulder, and at the same time she was still trying to dress herself.

51

Stone the Crows

A young girl and I were driving along a rural but very busy road one day. The girl in question was quite a hard-faced pupil; in other words, she was the sort of person who wouldn't take shit from anyone. We even had to stop several times on her driving lessons so she could have a fag or two. The sun was shining over the tops of the trees and I could just see the cattle grazing over the hedge rows in the beautiful green pastures. The birds were flying serenely in the sky and the crows were eating road kill. This one crow failed to understand how long it would take a car to stop at 60 mph, taking into account your thinking distance, braking distance, and overall stopping distance. The crow in question didn't get more than 18 inches off the ground on take-off before getting splattered by the front of our car. There was crow everywhere feathers flying around my windscreen and lots of other bits of crow that I would not like to describe. My pupil screamed out loud at the same time, gripping the steering wheel as hard has she could.

"Paul, Paul, I need to stop. Oh my God, what did I hit?"

"Don't worry," I said, trying to keep the situation calm, "it was just a little bird. I am sure it is okay."

"I need to stop and have a fag," she said. "I feel all shook up. I think I am going to cry." I noticed that her eyes were starting to water up and felt it better if we pulled over in a safe place.

We pulled over and we both went around the front of the car to see if there was any evidence of a bird strike. What a mess. The crow was unrecognisable, like something from a horror movie. My pupil almost passed out. She was now crying for Britain as I consoled her. I helped her to put her fag in her mouth, because she kept missing it.

All I needed now was for her to set herself on fire with her dodgy petrol lighter. She eventually calmed down, but asked me if I could drive her home. She might be hard on the outside, but inside she was as soft has a crow splattered in the grill of my car.

52

Examiners

Pupils generally have a misconception about driving test examiners, and at times I can understand why. As driving instructors we can all have a bit of a moan about why a pupil failed their test. Together we try to work as a team. We can all make mistakes at times, and as an instructor I know I have made my share. I remember sitting in on one of my pupils' driving tests. We were travelling along a dual carriageway when my pupil came across a tractor travelling at about 20 mph. I was thinking from the back of the car, *Please overtake the tractor, please, please, please overtake the tractor*. Not a chance.

She stayed behind the tractor for about a mile. I knew then that she would have failed her test for not making progress. It was only when we got back to the test centre and the examiner had left the vehicle that she said she had never been taught overtaking before. I was gob smacked and apologised to my pupil. I found it hard to believe that I had missed the subject out. She had failed on one other thing as well, which did soften the blow a bit. Examiners have never admitted to me that they have made mistakes, but to be fair, why would they? I don't think it would be doing them any favours.

I feel with examiners that some pupils will get the rub of the green while others will feel that they have been hard done by. I think that is just the nature of the test. The ones that pass can't praise the examiner enough, and the ones that don't pass either excepts it or in some cases kick off big time

Examiners with a sense of humour

Over years of being in the driving industry I have noticed that with all the changes, examiners have become more approachable, they seem to have developed a sense of humour that has been missing for years. It seems to settle the pupil down and stops them feeling so nervous. On one occasion my daughter had just returned from her driving test and I could see the examiner explaining something to her. I went over to the vehicle and was invited into the back to hear the debrief. The examiner turned to me and said, "I am sorry, Paul. She hasn't passed her test. I'm afraid she drove to close to a cyclist and almost knocked him off." I was gutted, until I saw my daughter look towards me with a grin on her face. I was still confused, until the examiner explained to me, "I am only joking. Your daughter drove really well. She as passed with only three driving faults." I just couldn't hold back from saying a few choice words to the examiner. Luckily for me the examiner had a great sense of humour and found it hilarious that she had got one over me.

On another occasion a young girl of mine was asked to open the bonnet of the car as part of the show-me/tell-me questions. As the examiner and the pupil both stood over the bonnet looking at the engine of the car, the examiner said, "I am going to ask you two questions as part of the show-me/tell-me questions, do you understand?"

"Yes," said my pupil.

"Okay," said the examiner. "The questions are to do with football."

"Explain the offside rule."

"What?" said the pupil. "I have no idea."

The examiner then said with a huge smile on his face, "I am only joking" and gave her the correct two questions.

On a third occasion my pupil came back from her driving test, and after turning her engine off the examiner said, "I am pleased to say that you have passed your driving test"

"What, me, are you sure?"

The examiner then said, "No, you haven't passed. I was only joking."

"Oh no," said my pupil.

The examiner then turned to my pupil and explained, "Of course you have passed your driving test. Your driving was excellent. There are just a few minor driving faults on the driving test report.

Examiners with Common Sense

There are times when common sense goes out of the window in all forms of life, so it is nice to see examiners put it to use at times. Examiners have a duty to check the car over before going out on test, and if they feel the car is not roadworthy they can refuse to carry out the test and the test fee will be lost.

I turned up at the test centre for my pupil's test, and after all the formalities the examiner and my pupil walked over to my car. I saw the examiner have a brief look around the car and then get in. I watched them as they drove off down the road and out of sight of the test centre. About 35 minutes later I saw them coming back and noticed that when my pupil pulled up on the left-hand side of the road, the back indicator was flashing at a very fast speed and the front one was not working at all. I knew then that the examiner would have known there was a problem with the indicator because it would have shown up on the dashboard. I went over to the car expecting my pupil to have failed her test. On reaching the car, the examiner opened the door for me to listen in to the debrief. I was shocked to hear the examiner say, "I am pleased to say you have passed your driving test. Could you pass me your driving licence please."

As the examiner was filling in the pass certificate, I said to the her, "Was there a problem with the indicators?"

"Yes, the left indicator was playing up."

"Oh," I said, "I thought you might have terminated the driving test."

The examiner then said, "Because your pupil drove so well, and the fact that the indicator stopped working within the last five minutes of the test, I managed to get her to drive back doing right turns only. I just used some common sense."

It was so nice to see common sense being used in this way.

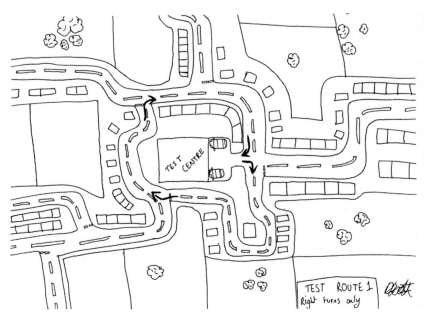

TEST ROUTE 1
Right turns only

On another occasion I was on the way to the test centre with my pupil on a cold, frosty morning when unexpectedly my door window fell into the door. I tried to wind it back up with my electric control, but it was having none of it. I was very concerned for my pupil knowing that his test might not take place. I said that we would carry on with the pre-hour and when we get to the test centre I would ask the examiner if he could still conduct the driving test.

On arrival, I saw the examiner walking back to the test centre from his first test of the day. I explained to the examiner the problem about the window. "I have tried everything to get the window up but its having none of it."

The examiner was a little concerned. "I will have to make a phone call to see if it will be okay for me to conduct the test. I am not happy about it, but I will see what I can do. Make your way to the test centre with your pupil and I will let you know in a minute what the outcome is."

My pupil and I waited with bated breath in the waiting room to see what the outcome would be. I heard the examiner coming out of his office, and I said to my pupil, "Well, we will know one way or the other in a few seconds."

The waiting room door opened. I looked over to the door and almost fell off my seat with laughter. The examiner was wearing a woollen hat stretched over his ears and a anorak type coat better suited to a train spotter, zipped up to his neck. The outfit was completed with an expensive pair of gloves.

He didn't need to tell me twice what his decision was. However, what he did say was "If it gets too cold whilst conducting the test I will have to terminate the driving test." I thought, with what he's wearing he could do the driving test on the top of mount Everest.

I decided to go along on the driving test just in case there was a sudden snow storm and the test got terminated. The test was completed, albeit a little cold for me in the back, but the pupil unfortunately failed his driving test. Three cheers for common sense.

Examiners with No Sense

I have tried to be as kind as I can so far; however, my kindness has now run dry. As instructors we all know that the examiners are in a no-win situation at times. If they pass your pupil then they are the best thing since sliced bread. If they don't pass your pupil then they are classed alongside the cockroaches. The tales that I am going to tell you have nothing to do with passing or failing your driving test; they have to do with the pupils just before going on their driving test.

I was taking a set of twins on their driving lessons, one boy and one girl. They were equals when it came to their ability to learn. I booked their driving tests for the same day the boys at 9:17 am. and the girls at 10:24 am. I picked them both up for their tests at the same time, which seemed to make more sense than going back to their house once the boy had taken his test. It was a cold, frosty morning, and I was a little concerned about the roads being a icy. We drove around for about forty-five minutes, taking in most of the roads around the test area. All the roads seemed fine with no signs of the test being cancelled. We then drove to the test centre and parked up our vehicle before taking in some nice, fresh air as we walked the final 50 metres in to the test centre's waiting room. We took our seats, and within minutes the examiner came out of his office and called the first of the twins over to do the paperwork before going out on their test.

The examiner politely asked what were the roads like outside.

"They are fine to my knowledge. My pupils and I have just been driving around most of the roads in the area, and we had no problem. We even did the emergency stop exercise, and that also went as well as can be expected, with no skidding of the wheels."

The examiner then said in a serious voice, "I think I better take a quick look outside to check for myself." I had no problem with that, knowing that the roads were free of any ice. The examiner then came back into the waiting room and asked me to accompany him outside. *What does he want to show me?* I thought. The examiner then said to me, "There are some ice patches in the gutter." He started to chip the ice away with the heel of his shoe and said, "I am not sure if i should cancel the test or not. What do you think?"

I said with a grumpy voice, "Does it matter what I think? You are the examiner, and you will make up your mind no matter what I say."

He said, "I need to take into account the pupils' safety when they are walking to the car."

You are having a laugh, I am thinking now. I said, "We have all just walked to the test centre without so much as a wobble."

The examiner said, "I am afraid I am going to have to cancel the driving test. I don't think the road conditions are suitable to conduct the test."

I couldn't even look at the examiner when he said he was cancelling the test. I just stormed into the test centre and said to my pupil in a very angry voice, "Let's go. The test has been cancelled. There is no point in hanging around here".

I just needed to get out of the test centre. On the way out I was passed by the examiner. I asked him, "Will the 10:24 test be taking place, or are you going to cancel that one as well?"

He said, "I cannot be sure at this moment in time. I shall after let you know when you arrive."

We all arrived back again for the 10:24 test. The examiner came out of his office and into the waiting room just like before. I was biting my bottom lip trying not to say anything sarcastic when the examiner said that he felt that the roads were now good enough to conduct the driving test. My pupil went on her driving test and passed on her first attempt. As for the boy, he came back a few weeks later and also passed the first time.

The next story is also about the same examiner. Maybe he didn't like me. Maybe the feeling is mutual. I turned up at the test centre with my female pupil. It was the last test of the day, at 3:27pm. It was very close to Christmas, so as you will know it goes dark very early on in the afternoon; normally by 4 pm. the driving test is just about finished. Anything any later than that would make it very difficult to complete the test. We sat in the waiting room awaiting the examiner, and at the same time I glanced at my watch to see what the time was. It was 3:27 pm., and there was still no sign of the examiner. A few minutes later I heard the examiner coming out of his office. It was now 3:30 pm., and with every second it was getting darker. The examiner introduced himself to my pupil and me. Then, after signing the declaration to say that the car was insured, he said, "There is something I need to say to you, and that is if you don't want to do the test this afternoon, you don't have to do it." He continued to say that earlier on this week I had a pupil that complained about the driving test. She said that it was too dark to see when she was reversing around a corner. "I have been instructed to inform all pupils on the last test of the day that if they don't want to do the test, they can cancel it and another test will be rescheduled for them."

We were both in agreement that we would like the test to be conducted. The examiner was now almost begging us to cancel it, saying, "Are you really sure you want to do the test, because once we walk out of that door there will be no turning back."

We said, "Yes, we understand."

"I will give you one last chance," said the examiner. "It's still not too late."

I thought, for God's sake, what part of *yes* do you not understand? The time was now 3:35 pm., and the examiner was not to happy that he could not persuade my pupil to change her mind. The examiner took to his heels and headed off towards my car with the pupil not too far behind him. I saw the examiner looking around my car for any defects; however, there was none to be found to his annoyance so what did he do? He came back into the waiting room and said, "Your lights need cleaning."

"The car was cleaned earlier on in the day."

"Not my problem," he said. "In my opinion, the lights need cleaning."

I managed to keep my calm and got some paper towels from the test centre toilet along with some water and cleaned the lights. The test started at about 3:40 pm. and was finished by 4:10 pm.

Oh, by the way, yes, you've guessed it, the pupil failed her driving test.

I think many instructors are quite pleased that this person no longer works has an examiner. He has moved on to greener pastures, I suppose.

53

Did Your Mum Never Tell You Not to Chase Cars

As driving instructors we do tend to get some abuse whilst on the roads from other road users, like hand signals that are not part of the Highway Code. Normally we can just laugh it off. If we didn't we would probably end up hanging our keys up and never instructing again.

My pupil and I were driving on a housing estate practising different skills. I said to my pupil to just pull over on the left in a safe and convenient place. Within minutes of pulling over, we were approached by about four or five young boys. They couldn't have been much older than ten or eleven. They were starting to annoy my pupil and me, so I wound down my window and asked them polity to go away. The abuse I got was not nice. One of the boys said, "You can't park here, so move your f***ing car before I tell my dad."

I was shocked to say the least and told the boy that I was allowed to park here, so will you please go away. He carried on with his abuse, so I just wound up my window and said to my pupil, "Start your engine and let's drive on when it is safe. I can't be doing with all this." Just then as we were about to move off, the boy in question decided to drop his trousers and do a Mooney against my window. All his mates were laughing and thought it was funny. Not a problem, I thought. I will see you again soon.

A few days later I was driving on the same estate and on the same road when I spotted the same boys again. I said to my pupil, "Don't stop, because I know these boys and they will just give us grief." As we were passing the boys they recognised me, and the one that had done the Mooney starting chasing my car at some speed. I could see his mates laughing in my rear-view mirror, they obviously thought it was amazingly funny. I said to my pupil in a calm and still voice, "I am going to give you an instruction now that I have not given you before, so just do what I say."

"Okay," said the pupil, "ready when you are."

"First of all, I would like you to take your right foot off the gas. Now hold on to the steering wheel tightly, as if you are crushing a grape, adopt a stiff upright position, check your rear-view mirror, and then finally smile."

I hit my dual -control brake as hard as I could, causing the car come to an abrupt stop. Within a split second there was a splat and a loud scream from the back of my car. The boy had hit my car and was now trying to pick himself up of the road. I checked my rear-view mirror again to see his friends all laughing. They were stunned by what had just happened. I got out of my car to check that my car had not suffered any damage. I gave the boy some grief for chasing my car and told him how stupid he was. I never did get any more grief from any of them.

54

Crime Watch

This story is of a more serious nature; however, looking back now I can see how some people would find it funny. I was at home one evening watching *Crime Watch* with my wife. They were showing a photo fit of a man who had committed a serious crime. I said to my wife, "My God, the photo fit looks just like me." My wife agreed, and we both thought no more about it.

About a week later I received a phone call whilst I was on a driving lesson from my driving school's office. The lady in the office said, "Hi, Paul, we need you to come into the office after you have finished your last driving lesson."

"Why, what's the problem?"

"You need to come to the office because the police want to talk to you."

Concerned, I said, "What do the police want with me?"

"They just need to talk to you about something or nothing," said the lady. I refused at first but then thought it would be in my own interest to go and see what they wanted to talk to me about. I felt a little nervous as I drove to my driving school's office, still trying to work out what crime I might have committed. The most trouble I had ever been in was getting a parking ticket.

I walked into the office, where I was asked to go into the back room. I was thinking, *Oh no, not the back room. I'm in serious trouble.* Two plain clothes policemen were there to interview me. They asked me questions like "Where were you on Tuesday the seventh of January?"

"No idea," I said. "Well, we have evidence to suggest that you were in this area on the date in question."

"Well then you must be right," I said, "I can't remember that far back."

After a few more questions to establish my whereabouts, I asked them, "Could you now tell me what this is all about?"

They agreed with the fact that they were pretty sure I was innocent. They said, "Someone had seen you driving around on your driving lessons, and they thought that you looked like someone they had seen on crime watch."

"It all falls in to place now", I said to the policemen. "Yes, I understand now. I was watching the program with my wife and said exactly the same thing." It was still quite ironic though: on the day in question I was in the area where the crime took place. In addition, the pupil I was teaching was a barrister; surely he could vouch for me.

I felt relieved that it all made sense now. My worst fears were over; however, I still had to spend three hours at the police station giving a statement, along with fingerprints and DNA. I do understand that the police do have a job to do and they must check all their leads. It has been at least fifteen years since I was taken in to the police station, so I think I would have heard something by now. Surely even the police can't be that slow.

55

Happy Days

Although as instructors we have dual-controlled cars, we are still very susceptible to the odd accident now and then. Some of the accidents just can't be avoided, like rear-end shunts. I myself have been involved in a few rear- end shunts in my time, just like lots of driving instructors on the road today. There was one accident I was involved in with my pupil that warranted my car being classified as a write-off. We were driving along a very windy country lane one morning. The weather was wet, and the roads were a little more challenging than if it had been a nice, dry, sunny day. My pupil and I were approaching a sharp left-hand bend, at the same time trying to keep as close as we could to the sandstone wall on our left. As we were about halfway around the sharp bend I noticed a large tuck driving towards us, taking up three quarters of the unmarked road. There was no room for us to pass the vehicle without hitting it. I hit the dual-control brake at the same time as I grabbed the steering wheel and pulled it to the left. The truck tried to steer away from us to avoid a collision, but to no avail. It collided with the off-side front of my car at the same time the near side of my car scraped along the sandstone wall, until it came to a halt.

There was hardly a scratch on the truck, but my car looked as if it had seen better days. The driver and I had an amicable chat about the accident, and we both agreed that it was a knock for knock accident, even though deep down inside I felt it was his fault for taking up three quarters of the road, and in his opinion, he thought it was my fault, thinking it was a little foolhardy of me to teach a pupil on such a narrow road.

My car was towed away to the local garage, and within a few days I was told the news that I was expecting, my car was a write-off. The first thing I was thinking now was how much the insurance company would be willing to pay me for my car. The figure that I came up with in my mind was about £7,700. The amount outstanding on my car was £6,000, so it meant that I would have enough money left over for a deposit on a new car. When I told my wife the figure that I thought would be acceptable in my mind, she said, "You have got to be joking. It's worth a lot more than that."

I disagreed and said, "Well, if you think you can get a better offer, then I will leave it for you to sort out."

While I was at work in my courtesy car, my wife phoned me to say, "They have offered you £8,200."

My first reaction was, "Well done, that's great. I really didn't think they would be willing to pay that amount."

My wife then said, "I still feel it is not enough, and I think I can get more if I push them harder."

I am now thinking I am more than happy with that amount, so I said to my wife, "Accept it."

"Not on your life," she said. "If I push them I am sure I can get more."

Again I said, "I think you should accept it, but I will leave it with you."

About an hour later my wife phoned and said, "I have spoken to someone from the insurance company and explained that we are not happy with that amount. The gentlemen at the other end said, 'I think that is a reasonable offer, madam. What sort of figure are you actually looking for?' I then said I told him I was thinking of more around £9,200. He then said in a shocked voice, 'What? I don't believe you are still asking for more.'"

"What did they say?" I asked.

"The gentleman I was talking to said there is no way he can make that decision on his own and he would need to talk to his manager. He is in a meeting at the moment, so when he comes out of the meeting, which will be in about an hour's time, I will speak to him and I will see what he says."

"Okay," I said. "Just let me know what they say when they phone you back."

My wife phoned me back to tell me the final outcome. "The same gentlemen phoned me back and said he had spoken to his manager and he wasn't willing to go above £10,500 and that would be their final offer. I thought about it for a few seconds and then said in a calm and ungrateful slow type of voice, 'Okay, then, if that's the best you can come up with, then on behalf of my husband I accept your offer.'"

I was gob smacked. HAPPY DAYS.

56

Trolley Walkout

The conversations you have with your pupils when on a driving lesson can cover any number of subjects depending on your pupil. Some of them like sport, some of them like to talk about their hobbies, and some like to discuss travel, TV, religion, family matters, etc. On this one occasion I was teaching a middle-aged gentlemen, and as we were driving along he suddenly said, "How can I become as good as you at driving?"

I said in a kind of intelligent manner, "It is important for you to listen very carefully to everything I say and for you to work as hard as you can on everything I have taught you." I continued, "I work really hard to be a top class driving instructor and I feel I am one of the best instructors around."

He said, "I am also the best at something."

I then said with curiosity, "What is it that you feel you are the best at?"

He replied, "Trolley walkout. I am the best at it. In fact, it was me who invented it."

Still very confused about what he had said I asked him to explain.

"What you do is you go to a supermarket and take an empty trolley in to the store with you. You then fill the trolley up with as much stuff has you can. You then pick your moment, and leg it as fast as you can out of the store to a car that's waiting for you. You then make your getaway."

I was stunned and said to him, "You have got to be joking me."

"No, I am not joking. The last time I did a trolley walkout I got away with twelve bottles of malt whiskey and twelve of Champagne."

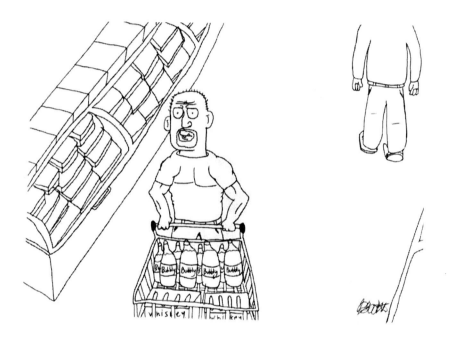

After what he had told me I thought it best not to drive too close to any supermarkets in the future. I eventually had a massive fallout with this gentlemen over other issues, and I refused to teach him any more.

57

You Can't Park There

You can't park there. Well, that depends on who you are. I was talking to an examiner just after he had taken a pupil on his driving test. Apparently the pupil was on his way back to the test centre, and within about twenty metres of the finishing line when he noticed a vehicle parked on the left-hand side of the road by the junction he was trying to drive out of. The parked vehicle was causing the pupil difficulty seeing around it and into the new road he needed to turn into. None too happy, the pupil spoke out loudly with the examiner sat beside him, "What stupid idiot parks his car that close to a junction? I can't see a thing."

The examiner looked at the pupil and said in a shocked voice, "That's my car."

The pupil went silent for a few seconds before apologising to the examiner. The examiner took it with a pinch of salt and actually found it quite funny. The pupil still passed his driving test. After all, it wasn't his fault that the examiner didn't know the correct distance to park his car from a junction.

58

Like Mother Like Daughter

A young girl I was taking on driving lessons ended up being one of the rudest girls I have ever had the displeasure in taking. If my pupil made any kind of fault that I couldn't sort out on the move I would instruct her to pull over at the side of the road in a safe and convenient place to discuss the faults. This would normally be straightforward practice, but not on this occasion e. Every time I tried to explain to her the reasons behind the fault all she would say is "Fine, I understand, can we now get on with the driving?" I was quite taken back by her attitude and tried to explain to her that I hadn't finished with my explanation. She was not interested in what I had to say and continued bombarding me with abuse. "I want to drive. Now will you stop wasting my time? I have understood where I went wrong, so why won't you let me drive?" It was quite obvious to me at this moment in time, this girl was going to struggle to pass her driving test. I told her to drive on when it was safe to do so, and to be honest I wasn't even remotely concerned about whether she had understood what I had tried to explained to her. After a few more driving lessons of much of the same thing, not wanting to listen to anything I had to say, I met her mum for the first time.

I got out of my car at the end of her driving lesson to be confronted by this lady who was walking up her garden path towards me at some pace. When she finally got to me she said to me in a very abrupt voice, "I would like to discuss my daughter's progress with you, please. I would like to know how her driving is progressing."

I said to her, "It's not her driving I am concerned about. It's her attitude towards being taught."

Her mum said to me, "I am not interested in my daughter's attitude; I am just interested in her driving."

I repeated what I had said, thinking she might listen to me second time around. Not a chance. "I told you, and I won't tell you again, I am not interested in my daughter's attitude. I am only interested in her driving."

I was shocked but not surprised at her mum's attitude. I tried to explain to my pupil's mum without mentioning the word attitude again that her driving was satisfactory but needed some attention. I never did see her mum again. Lucky, lucky me. Her daughter took her driving test and failed within the first minute. I explained to her that when you drive out of the test centre car park you must make sure you keep over to the left-hand side of the road. Some pupils think that it is like a one-way system where you would keep to the right for a right turn. Did she listen? Out of the car park she drove straight over to the right hand side of the road. I never saw her again. Lucky, lucky me.

59

Skid Marks

I had a pupil I was taking on driving lessons that was rather heavy footed. I taught him the emergency stop exercise on one of his driving lessons, and even after weeks of practising the emergency stop he still couldn't brake without the wheels of the car locking up. On the day of his test I practised all of his manoeuvres, including the emergency stop exercise, in the pre-hour before his test. All manoeuvres went well and has usual the emergency stop exercise went tits up. In fact, the skid marks were getting progressively longer. I think we started off with skid marks that were about a foot in length, and now we were at the stage where they were pushing about a metre. Just before we went into the test centre for him to take his test, I had one final word for him: "Please brake gently when you carry out the emergency exercise."

After all the formalities had taken place in the test centre, the examiner took my pupil for his driving test. I decided to take a walk to the local shop to buy a coffee with one of the other driving instructors. We both saw our pupils drive off around the block and out of sight. Just then I said to the other driving instructor, "There is nothing we can do now. They're on their own. I just hope they pass."

The instructor said he felt his pupil should pass, but you never know. I replied, "My pupil was a very good driver, but his emergency stop exercise needs some attention." At this point we both heard the loudest screeching of tyres that we have ever heard. We were both waiting for the bang that normally follows the screeching. No bang ever materialised. I thought, that's odd, until it suddenly dawned on me. *Please don't let that be my pupil carrying out the emergency stop exercise.*

I had a nervous wait of about thirty minutes before I would find out the outcome. Both pupils arrived back at the test centre at about the same time, and as I was walking over to my car I could see by looking through the window that my pupil had passed his test. Once the examiner had left the vehicle I went over to my pupil to congratulate him on passing on his first attempt.

"Just tell me one thing that wasn't you was it carrying out the emergency stop exercise at the back of the test centre."

"Yes, it was. Why, did you hear it?"

"Heard it, I could smell the rubber of the tyres burning on the tarmac. How the hell did you manage to pass?"

"The examiner said my overall driving was very good, so he would take all that into account."

I explained to him on another day he could have easily have failed his driving test. I drove past where my pupil had carried out his emergency stop exercise, and on first inspection it was quite obvious that this was by far his best one yet. I would say that the skid marks were at least four to five feet in length.

60

And Finally

I was parked up with my pupil on a hot summer morning when we saw two ladies cycling towards us. One of them was cycling in the middle of the road with her daughter, and the other one seemed to be on crack cocaine, with the way she was all over the road. I spotted a young girl cycling on the pavement in front us but behind the two ladies. The young girl couldn't seem to get past the rubbish bin that was blocking her path, as there was a car parked alongside the bin. I saw that she was crying. Then her mum, who was completely unaware of the situation, suddenly noticed as she looked around over her shoulder that her daughter was in distress. The lady went over to her daughter and shouted at her before getting hold of the bin and throwing it to one side with some force.

If I hadn't had known better I would have thought she was putting her name forward for the next vacancy to be a bin man, or should I say bin woman's. I would have definitely given her the job after what I saw. The young girl cycled past us still on the pavement, still crying. I said to my pupil, "What a horrible woman."

My pupil looked at me and said, "Around here she is what is known as a scummy mummy."

I just fell about laughing. I had never heard that saying before, but you know what? My pupil was absolutely correct. "Scummy mummy."

Fancy a game of tick? Well, I certainly wouldn't want a game of tick in the area I was driving in with my pupil. I was having a general chat with my pupil has we drove around a slightly rough area. I noticed a few young lads walking on the kerb that looked to me like the sort I wouldn't want to hang around with. I said to my pupil I wouldn't want to live or hang around this area, as it looked a little rough for my liking. I was actually searching for some feedback given that my pupil lived close by, and I was thinking that you shouldn't judge a book by its cover maybe I was wrong in my judgement. I was not wrong. My pupil said, "Rough? You don't know the half of it. It's so rough around here that they play tick with baseball bats." I laughed so much we had to pull over and stop. I had this vision in my mind of these lads hitting each other over the head with baseball bats. Whack, you're on.

It's amazing how much you can learn from your pupils some good, some bad, and some just laughable. My pupil and I were driving along a road that was 30 mph when suddenly my pupil spotted the National Speed Limit Sign. I didn't say anything about what the sign means, as she was an experienced driver. My pupil then said with a huge smile on her face, "At last, the GLF sign."

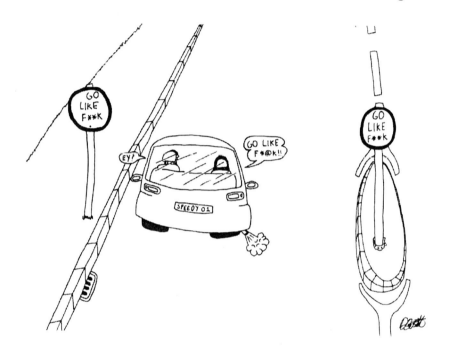

"Sorry, what did you say?" I asked, thinking she was talking a load of testicles.

"At last, the GLF sign."

I said, "I am confused. I have never heard of a GLF sign."

"I don't think it's in the Highway Code, but it means Go Like F**k."

Absolutely brilliant, you learn something every day.

My pupil and I were stopped at a red traffic light when a car rolled up alongside us in the right-hand lane and also stop at the lights. I thought it would be a good time to ask my pupil a question whilst we were stationary. I said to her, "When the lights change to green, who would go first?" The answer I was looking for was that we would both go at the same time. The answer she gave me was, "They would go first." I am now thinking got cha, so I asked my pupil, "Why do you think they go first?" She said, "Because I always stall it."

A classic answer. Credit where credit's due.

Sometimes you get pupils that seem to have a language of their own. I have been blessed with all kinds of words and phrases. On one lesson, I had a young boy who was a country boy that drove tractors. His driving was excellent; however, his word choice wasn't. We were driving along a road one day when suddenly he came out with "That's the badger."

I said what the heck does that mean. He said that it is like agreeing with something that you have said or done. From that day onwards every time my pupil did something well, I kept finding myself saying, "That's the badger." I have been brainwashed.

Who the f**k is One Direction? I was in the test centre on December 30, 2011, with my pupil. As we walked in and took a seat I looked across the room to see that another instructor was there with his pupil. The instructor asked me how I was and how was business these days. I said fine, thank you for asking. There are frequently awkward silences in the test centre. It's like being in the doctor's waiting room. So the instructor's pupil decided to break the ice my saying to me, "You look a bit stressed out."

I wasn't sure what to make of his comment. Was he trying to be a bit of a smart arse, or was he was just trying to make conversation with me? I took it as if he was being a little intrusive, so I responded with a few choice words.

"It's pupils like yourself that stress us instructors out."

"What do you mean?"

"When pupils don't do what you ask them to do, even when you have taught them the same thing over and over again. I think you would look stressed out if you were in my shoes."

He turned to his instructor and said, "I don't stress you out, do I?"

His instructor said, "No, of course you don't."

I felt as if I had been a little rude to him, so I said, "No, I didn't mean it in that way. I am sure you and my pupil will do extremely well on your test." He thanked me for my kind words.

Just then, the examiners came out to take them both on their driving tests. The other instructor decided that he would go on the driving test with his pupil, so I just waited in the test centre on my own for them both to come back from their driving test.

The other examiner came back first off their driving test, and I could see by the excitement that the pupil had passed his test. He got out of the car and was having his photograph taken with his instructor. It seemed a bit strange but not completely unheard of. I saw my pupil approaching the test centre just has the other examiner was walking back to where I was standing. The examiner said to me, "You see that young man over there who has just passed his test?" I said yes. "Well, he said he is going to buy himself a Lamborghini."

I said, "Wow, that's okay for some. I take it he is rich."

The examiner then said, "Have you ever heard of One Direction?"

"I don't think so. Are they a mobile phone company or something like that?" I was thinking that maybe his dad owned a mobile phone company.

The examiner said, "No, they are a pop group that were on the *X Factor*." I still had no idea who he was or who One Direction were. He then said, "His name is Harry Styles."

"Oh right," I said. "I shall tell my daughter when I get back home. She is eighteen, so she might know him." I went over to my car where my pupil had also passed his driving test, I told the story to my pupil, and his response was, "I thought it was Harry Styles, but didn't like to say just in case I was wrong."

On arriving home I explained to my daughter the story, and she was gutted I didn't get his autograph. I have since looked them up on You Tube, and to be honest I thought they were really good. Sorry, Harry, if I sounded a little rude and well done on passing your driving test.

I arrived at my pupil's house on the morning of her driving test. I was a little early, so I decided to wait in the car. The next thing, her mum came out of the front door and said to me in a kind of sharp voice, "You are too early. She is not ready yet. You should know better than to turn up for a lady early."

I'm thinking, *Lady* . . . (I could think of a few names for her, but Lady isn't one of them). She continued, "I will go and hurry her up." Then she closed the front door.

As the front door was closing I saw my pupil walking by the side of the house. She had come from around the back of her house. She must have heard the front door close, and she asked me, "Was that my mother?" I said yes. My pupil then said, "What did my mum want?" I was afraid to say too much, because I know how explosive my pupil could be, so I tried to play it down.

"She just wanted to wish you good luck."

My pupil could see straight through me, so she went back inside to have a go at her mum. When she came back I said, "What did you say to your mum?"

"I told her to pick her window."

She failed her test and I never saw her again. You see, some stories do have a happy ending at least for me anyway.

Mirrors are always a major concern on the driving test, so as instructors we have to be really keen that the pupils check the mirrors at the correct time. It was a really hot day and I was watching my pupil quite closely to make sure she checked her mirrors properly. I noticed that she did a really good off-side mirror check as we were driving along, so I praised her for the check. "Well done. That was a really nice mirror check."

"I didn't check my mirror," she said.

"You did. I just saw you look over to the right, checking your off-side mirror."

"I wasn't checking my mirror," she said. "I was looking at that man over there with the six-pack."

I did find it funny but also slightly frustrating, given that I don't have a six-pack (any more).

I was reversing around a corner with a female pupil, and as part of the brief I will tell them, if it ain't broke don't fix it. This will normally stop them from over-steering or steering when then don't need to. I thought on this one occasion I would get the pupil to fill in the blank, basically trying to see if she knew what the missing word would be, so I said to her, "If it ain't broke, don't . . . ?"

Then I paused, waiting for the missing word.

It took awhile until I got the response: "Choke."

"Sorry," I said.

"If it ain't broke, don't choke."

I just shook my head and grinned. If that was the case, I would have no pupils left. They would have all choked to death.

I confess to being a bit of an extrovert at times; however, when I turned up for my pupil one morning, I was greeted by my pupil's mum filming me as I drove into their drive. I got out of the, car and it was like doing an interview for the ITN News.

She was pointing the camera in to my face, talking into the camera saying things like, "This is my son's driving instructor. My son has got his first driving lesson today." I just smiled at the camera. My pupil came out to join me on camera. That made me feel better now, as I was not on my own getting all the limelight. "This is my son getting into the passenger seat, and the instructor is now going to drive him away to a quiet area to start his lesson." I felt like saying, "This is the driving instructor, and I am going to smash your video camera if you don't stop filming me." We left the film studios to go to a more discreet area out of the way of all the cameras.

After the lesson I said to my pupil, "I think it's time we head back to the film studios. Would you like to drive, or would you like me to take over?" He agreed to drive us back, and as we turned into his road, you guessed it, the camera was out again. I said, "Try not to look at the camera. Just turn left on to your drive. I will take control to stop you stalling it if I need to. You never know. We might be on the Northwest news tonight, so try not to embarrass yourself." We managed to stop the car without stalling it, and I even managed a little wave at the camera. It is nice to know now that I am tucked away in someone's video archive.

For all you young students out there, I am pretty sure that you will find this funny. I was taking three young lads on some driver training at their local school. They were all sixteen years of age, so they could only drive in the school grounds and not on the roads. It was a marketing tool aimed at bringing in more work when they turned seventeen. There was only so much we could do in the small, confined area we could do some figure-of-eight turnings, stopping and moving away, hill starts, and there was just enough room to do the emergency stop exercise. It was a six-week course, and each lesson was an hour long; that meant each of the three pupils I had in my car got to drive for about twenty minutes each. It was the last week of their six-week course, and I allowed them to do any of the subjects we had covered over the last six weeks. Each one of them wanted to do the emergency stop exercise. Now, why didn't that surprise me? It was all going well, until this one lad decided to go a little faster than his mates did. I felt it was just about a safe speed, but when he hit the brakes the wheels locked up and the car skidded straight through the wooden boiler house doors. We were all shocked, and it wasn't long before the headmaster came out to see the damage.

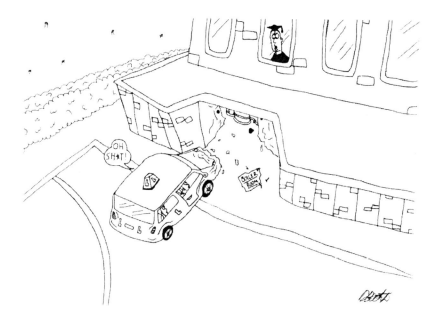

He was not amused and said, "If that had happened a couple of minutes earlier you would have taken the caretaker out, because he was sitting behind the doors having a cup of tea." The students, to be honest, were laughing. You can't blame them. I had to try to keep a straight face and explain to the headmaster that I think there's a good possibility you will need a new set of boiler house doors.

Sometimes you will get parents phoning you up to book driving lessons for their sons and daughters but wanting to keep it a surprise. I had one lady who phoned me up and said that her son was seventeen in two weeks time and she wanted to surprise him on his birthday with a driving lesson. She surprised him all right. I got a phone call on the day in question to say, "My son has gone ballistic now he has found out that he is due to have a driving lesson today. I just can't believe it. I thought he would have loved to have a driving lesson on his birthday. He his refusing point blank to have the lesson and is saying he doesn't feel ready for driving."

I did say I would go round and sort him out, but his mum thought it best I didn't.

My pupil and I were driving along a 40 mph road when I noticed her speed creeping up just above the forty mark. I said to her, "Be careful of your speed, because you sometimes get the police on roads like this with their speed gun."

After a pause of a few seconds my pupil said, "Why would the police have a gun to catch you speeding? Surely that would be dangerous."

I explained, "It is not a real gun. They are not going to shoot you if you break the speed limit."

I instructed my pupil to pull over in a safe and convenience place whereupon she hit the kerb has she was stopping. After the car had come to a stop I looked over to my pupil and said in a kind of amusing way "you made a right cock up of that didn't you" she responded by saying "i like a good cock up" I said "what did you say" she repeated "i like a cock up", I was lost for words and just told her to drive on when it is safe to do so.

There are some occasions when your pupil will ask if they can do the driving lesson in then own car. On this one occasion, I said to my pupil that would be fine, since her driving was at an advanced stage. We were approaching a mini roundabout with minimal traffic around us when I said to her, "Turn left at the roundabout please." There seemed to be no danger at all. She approached the roundabout, keeping to the left hand side of the road, and had her left indicator on. On entering the roundabout we started to turn left, and we were just about to exit the roundabout when she suddenly decided to turn the steering wheel to the right and take the straight ahead exit. I could see that we were now in trouble, as a car had entered the roundabout in front of us thinking we were turning left. My first reaction was to go for the dual control brake. My leg was going up and down like a fiddler's elbow trying to find the brake. Then it dawned on me that I didn't have one. I shouted to my pupil, "Brake," but she just froze. Smash, straight into the side of the car we went. I explained to the driver of the other car that it was totally our fault, even though the rule is give way to traffic on the right. I think it would have taken a bloody good lawyer to get us acquitted of any blame on this occasion.

A pupil of mine phoned me up one day to say that he would be able to do a driving lesson any time next week because he had been suspended for a week. I asked him, "What on earth have you been up to being suspended for a week?"

He said, "I took a photo of the teacher's car and advertised it on e Bay with a starting price of 1p. I also put the schools phone number on the listing, so anyone that was interested in the car could phone up the school to make the teacher an offer for his car. The teacher was receiving phone calls all day long and was demanding the culprit own up to their crime. Unfortunately for me, someone dobbed me in to the teacher, and I got a week's suspension."

Lightning Source UK Ltd.
Milton Keynes UK
UKOW040121231012

200987UK00001B/38/P